Architecting for Scale
High Availability for Your Growing Applications

Lee Atchison

Beijing · Boston · Farnham · Sebastopol · Tokyo

Architecting for Scale

by Lee Atchison

Printed in the United States of America.

Published by O'Reilly Media, Inc., 1005 Gravenstein Highway North, Sebastopol, CA 95472.

O'Reilly books may be purchased for educational, business, or sales promotional use. Online editions are also available for most titles (*http://safaribooksonline.com*). For more information, contact our corporate/institutional sales department: 800-998-9938 or *corporate@oreilly.com*.

Editor: Brian Anderson	**Indexer:** WordCo Indexing Services, Inc.
Production Editor: Nicholas Adams	**Interior Designer:** David Futato
Copyeditor: Bob Russell, Octal Publishing, Inc.	**Cover Designer:** Karen Montgomery
Proofreader: Jasmine Kwityn	**Illustrator:** Rebecca Demarest

July 2016:   First Edition

Revision History for the First Edition
2016-07-07:   First Release

See *http://oreilly.com/catalog/errata.csp?isbn=9781491943397* for release details.

978-1-491-94339-7

[LSI]

To Beth

Table of Contents

Part II. Risk Management

Part VI. Conclusion

Foreword

We are living in interesting times, a software Cambrian explosion if you will, where the cost of building new systems has fallen by orders of magnitude and the connectivity of systems has grown by equal orders of magnitude. Resources like Amazon's AWS, Microsoft's Azure, and Google's GCP make it possible for us to physically scale our systems to sizes that we could only have imagined a few years ago.

The economics of these resources and seemingly limitless capacity is producing a uniquely rapid radiation of new ideas, new products, and new markets in ways that were never possible before. But all of these new explorations are only possible if the systems we build can scale. While it is easier than ever to build something small, building a system that can scale quickly and reliably proves to be a lot harder than just spinning up more hardware and more storage.

Software systems go through a predictable lifecycle starting with small well-crafted solutions fully understood by a single person, through the rapid growth into a monolith of technical debt, thence fissioning into an ad hoc collection of fragile services, and finally into a well-engineered distributed system able to scale reliably in both breadth (more users) and depth (more features). It's easy to see what needs to be done from the outside (make it more reliable!) and much harder to see the path from the inside. Fortunately, this book is the essential guidebook for the journey—from availability to service tiers, from game days to risk matrices, Lee describes the key decisions and practices for systems that scale.

Lee joined me at New Relic when we were first moving from being a single product monolith into being a multiproduct company, all while enjoying the hyper-growth in satisfied customers that made New Relic so successful. Lee came with a lot of experience at Amazon, both on the retail side where they grew a lot and on the AWS side where—guess what?—they grew a lot. Lee has been part of teams and led teams and been actively involved in a whole lot of scaling and he has the scars to prove it. Fortunately for us, he's lived through the mistakes and suffered through fiendishly difficult outages and is now passing along those lessons so that we don't have to get those same scars.

When Lee joined New Relic, we were suffering through our awkward teenage fail whale years. Our primitive monolith was suffering from our success and our availability, reliability, and performance was not good. By putting in place the techniques he's written about in this book, we graduated from those high school years and built the robust enterprise-level service that exists today. One of our tools was establishing four levels of availability engineering: Bronze, Silver, Gold, and Platinum. To earn the Bronze level, a team had to have a risk matrix, have defined SLAs. To earn the Silver level, a team had to be monitoring for the problems identified in the matrix and be using game days; Gold meant that the risks were mitigated; and Platinum was like a CMM Level 5 where the systems were self-healing and the focus was on continuous improvement. We prioritized these efforts for the Tier 1 services first, then the Tier 2 services, etc and we eventually got everyone to at least Silver and most of the teams through Gold (and a couple to Platinum).

When I moved to InVision App, I joined a younger company, again moving through the transition from early success to hyper growth, and thus I'm driving forward all these same techniques and tools that Lee describes. I urge you, in your journey as part of this exciting explosion of new systems and products and companies, to do the same: to learn from Lee in building your systems for scale.

— Bjorn Freeman-Benson, Ph.D., CTO
InVision App

Preface

As applications grow, two things begin to happen: they become significantly more complicated (and hence brittle), and they handle significantly larger traffic volume (which more novel and complex mechanisms manage). This can lead to a death spiral for an application, with users experiencing brownouts, blackouts, and other quality-of-service and availability problems.

But your customers don't care. They just want to use your application to do the job they expect it to do. If your application is down, slow, or inconsistent, customers will simply abandon it and seek out competitors that can handle their business.

This book helps you avoid the aforementioned death spiral by teaching you basic techniques that you can utilize to build and manage your large-scale applications. Once you've mastered these skills, your applications will be able to reliably handle huge quantities of traffic as well as huge variability in traffic without affecting the quality your customers expect.

Who Should Read This Book

This book is intended for software engineers, architects, engineering managers, and directors who build and operate large-scale applications and systems. If you manage software developers, system reliability engineers, or DevOps engineers, or you run an organization that contains large-scale applications and systems, the suggestions and guidance provided in this book will help you make your applications run smoother and more reliably.

If your application started small and has seen incredible growth (and is now suffering from some of the growing pains associated with that growth), you might be suffering from reduced reliability and reduced availability. If you struggle with managing technical debt and associated application failures, this book will provide guidance in reducing that technical debt to make your application able to handle larger scale more easily.

Why I Wrote This Book

After spending many years at Amazon building highly scaled applications in both the retail and the Amazon Web Services (AWS) worlds, I moved to New Relic, which was in the midst of hyper growth. The company felt the pain of needing the systems and processes required to manage highly scaled applications, but hadn't yet fully developed the processes and disciplines to scale its application.

At New Relic, I saw firsthand the struggles of a company going through the process of trying to scale, and realized that there were many other companies experiencing the same struggles every day.

My intent with this book is to help others working in these hyper-growth applications learn processes and best practices that can assist them in avoiding the pitfalls awaiting them as they scale.

Whether your application is growing tenfold or just 10 percent each year, whether the growth is in number of users, number of transactions, amount of data stored, or code complexity, this book can help you build and maintain your application to handle that growth, while maintaining a high level of availability.

A Word on Scale Today

Cloud-based services are growing and expanding at extremely high speeds. Software as a Service (SaaS) is becoming the norm for application development, primarily because of the need for providing these cloud-based services. SaaS applications are particularly sensitive to scaling issues due to their multitenant nature.

As our world changes and we focus more and more on SaaS services, cloud-based services, and high-volume applications, scaling becomes increasingly important. There does not seem to be an end in sight to the size and complexity to which our cloud applications can grow.

The very mechanisms that are state of the art today for managing scale will be nothing more than basic tenants tomorrow, and the solutions to tomorrow's scaling issues will make today's solutions look simplistic and minimalistic. Our industry will demand more and more complex systems and architectures to handle the scale of tomorrow.

The intent with this book is to provide content that stands the test of time.

Navigating This Book

Managing scale is not only about managing traffic volume—it also involves managing risk and availability. Often, all these things are different ways of describing the same problem, and they all go hand in hand. Thus, to properly discuss scale, we must also consider availability, risk management, and modern architecture paradigms such as microservices and cloud computing.

As such, this book is organized as follows:

Part I, "Availability"

Availability and availability management are often the first areas that are affected when an application begins to scale.

Chapter 1, What Is Availability?
> To begin, we'll establish what high availability means and how it differs from reliability.

Chapter 2, Five Focuses to Improve Application Availability
> In this chapter, I provide five core areas to focus on in building your application in order to improve its availability.

Chapter 3, Measuring Availability
> This chapter describes a standard algorithm for measuring availability and further explores the meaning of high availability.

Chapter 4, Improving Your Availability When It Slips
> If your application is suffering from availability problems (or you want to make sure it never does), we provide some organization-level steps you can take to help you improve your application's availability.

Part II, "Risk Management"

Understanding risk in your system is essential to improving availability as well as enhancing your application's ability to scale to the high levels needed today and in the future.

Chapter 5, What Is Risk Management?
> This chapter opens the topic of managing risk with highly scaled applications by outlining the basics of what risk management is all about.

Chapter 6, Likelihood Versus Severity
> This chapter discusses the difference between severity of a risk occurring and the likelihood of it occurring. They are both important, but in different ways.

Chapter 7, The Risk Matrix
> In this chapter, I present a system designed for helping you understand and manage the risk within your application.

Chapter 8, Risk Mitigation

> This chapter discusses how to take known risks within your system and reduce the impact they have on your application.

Chapter 9, Game Days

> This chapter looks at ongoing testing and evaluation of your risk-management plans, mitigation plans, and disaster plans. It reviews the techniques for doing this in production environments and the advantage of doing so.

Chapter 10, Building Systems with Reduced Risk

> In this chapter, I give suggestions on how to reduce risk within your applications and build applications with lower risk.

Part III, "Services and Microservices"

Services and microservices are an architecture strategy for building larger and more complicated applications that need to operate at higher scale.

Chapter 11, Why Use Services?

> This chapter explores why services are important to building highly scalable applications.

Chapter 12, Using Microservices

> Here, I provide an introduction on creating microservice-based architectures, focusing on sizing of services and determining where service boundaries should be created in order to improve scaling and availability.

Chapter 13, Dealing with Service Failures

> In the final chapter of this part, we'll discuss how to build services to handle failures.

Part IV, "Scaling Applications"

Scaling is not just about traffic, it's about your organization and how it responds to larger application needs.

Chapter 14, Two Mistakes High

> This chapter describes how to scale your system to maintain high availability, even in light of other failures.

Chapter 15, Service Ownership

> This chapter looks at how paying attention to ownership of services can help your organization and application scale.

Chapter 16, Service Tiers

> This chapter describes a way of labeling the criticalness of your services that helps manage service expectations.

Chapter 17, Using Service Tiers
> After defining service tiers, we put them to use to help manage the impact of service failures, responsiveness requirements, and expectation management.

Chapter 18, Service-Level Agreements
> In this chapter, we'll discuss using SLAs as a way of managing interdependence between service owners.

Chapter 19, Continuous Improvement
> This chapter provides techniques and guidelines for how to improve the overall scalability of your application.

Part V, "Cloud Services"

Cloud-based services are becoming increasingly important in building and managing large, critical applications with significant scaling requirements.

Chapter 20, Change and the Cloud
> This chapter explores the ways cloud computing has changed how we think about building highly scaled web applications.

Chapter 21, Distributing the Cloud
> This chapter outlines how to effectively use regions and availability zones to improve availability and scale.

Chapter 22, Managed Infrastructure
> This chapter describes how you can use managed services such as RDS, SQS, SNS, and SES to scale your application and reduce management load.

Chapter 23, Cloud Resource Allocation
> Here, we discuss how cloud resources are allocated and the implications of different allocation techniques on your application's scalability.

Chapter 24, Scalable Computing Options
> This chapter looks at highly scalable programming models such as AWS Lambda, which you can use to improve scaling, availability, and application manageability.

Chapter 25, AWS Lambda
> The final chapter in this part provides a more in-depth exploration of AWS Lambda, a technology that offers extremely high scalability options for events with simple computational requirements.

Part VI, "Conclusion"

Chapter 26, Putting It All Together
This chapter pulls together the major topics from each of the previous sections into a simple summary, which can be read as a reminder of what was covered in each chapter.

Online Resources

The Architecting for Scale website (*http://www.architectingforscale.com*) offers additional information about this book, including links to the supplementary material (*http://bit.ly/architectbookdl*). You can find more information about me on my website (*http://www.leeatchison.com*), and you can also follow my blog (*http://bit.ly/leeatscale*).

Conventions Used in This Book

The following typographical conventions are used in this book:

Italic
Indicates new terms, URLs, email addresses, filenames, and file extensions.

`Constant width`
Used for program listings, as well as within paragraphs to refer to program elements such as variable or function names, databases, data types, environment variables, statements, and keywords.

`Constant width bold`
Shows commands or other text that should be typed literally by the user.

`Constant width italic`
Shows text that should be replaced with user-supplied values or by values determined by context.

This icon signifies a tip or suggestion.

This element signifies a general note.

This icon indicates a warning or caution.

Safari® Books Online

 *Safari Books Online* is an on-demand digital library that delivers expert content in both book and video form from the world's leading authors in technology and business.

Technology professionals, software developers, web designers, and business and creative professionals use Safari Books Online as their primary resource for research, problem solving, learning, and certification training.

Safari Books Online offers a range of plans and pricing for enterprise, government, education, and individuals.

Members have access to thousands of books, training videos, and prepublication manuscripts in one fully searchable database from publishers like O'Reilly Media, Prentice Hall Professional, Addison-Wesley Professional, Microsoft Press, Sams, Que, Peachpit Press, Focal Press, Cisco Press, John Wiley & Sons, Syngress, Morgan Kaufmann, IBM Redbooks, Packt, Adobe Press, FT Press, Apress, Manning, New Riders, McGraw-Hill, Jones & Bartlett, Course Technology, and hundreds more. For more information about Safari Books Online, please visit us online.

How to Contact Us

Please address comments and questions concerning this book to the publisher:

O'Reilly Media, Inc.
1005 Gravenstein Highway North
Sebastopol, CA 95472
800-998-9938 (in the United States or Canada)
707-829-0515 (international or local)
707-829-0104 (fax)

We have a web page for this book, where we list errata, examples, and any additional information. You can access this page at *http://bit.ly/architecting-for-scale*.

To comment or ask technical questions about this book, send email to *bookquestions@oreilly.com*.

For more information about our books, courses, conferences, and news, see our website at *http://www.oreilly.com*.

Find us on Facebook: *http://facebook.com/oreilly*

Follow us on Twitter: *http://twitter.com/oreillymedia*

Watch us on YouTube: *http://www.youtube.com/oreillymedia*

Acknowledgments

While there are more people who helped make this book possible than I could possibly ever list here, I do want to mention several people specifically who were particularly helpful to me:

- Bjorn Freeman-Benson, who supported me significantly in the early stages of developing this book, and who gave me opportunities at New Relic that helped provide me the insights I needed for this book.

- Kevin McGuire, who has been a friend and confidant. We started at New Relic together, and it was his foresight and imagination that has helped give my career the needed focus and direction that guides me today.

- Natasha Litt, who has been a good friend and provided much encouragement and support.

- Jade Rubick, who with his constant smile and positive outlook, has provided me well-reasoned advice and guidance. What a great friend to have.

- Jim Gochee, who introduced me to the magic that was New Relic, both as a product and eventually as a career.

- Lew Cirne, whose vision has given us New Relic, and me a career and a home. The joy and driven enthusiasm you get after meeting with Lew one on one is highly infectious and hugely empowering. No wonder New Relic is so successful.

- Abner Germanow, Jay Fry, Bharath Gowda, and Robson Grieve, who took a chance on me and fought to get me my current role at New Relic. Who says you can't take a square peg and put it into a round hole? And have it actually fit! This is, by far, the most fun, rewarding, and personally fulfilling role I have ever had.

- Mikey Butler, Nic Benders, Matthew Flaming, and the rest of the New Relic engineering leadership, for all of their support over the years.

- Kurt Kufeld, who mentored me and helped me fit into the weird, chaotic, challenging, draining, and ultimately hugely rewarding work environment at Amazon.

- Greg Hart, Scott Green, Patrick Franklin, Suresh Kumar, Colin Bodell, and Andy Jassy, who gave me opportunities at Amazon and AWS I could not have ever imagined.

- Brian Anderson, my editor, who took a chance on me in writing this book, and helped me every step of the way.

I would like to give a very special acknowledgment to Abner Germanow and Bjorn Freeman-Benson. They both made it possible for me to work on this book. This book would not, could not, have happened without their support. For that, I will always be grateful.

To my family, and especially my wife Beth, who is my constant light and guide through this life we have together. My days are brighter, and my path is clearer, because she is with me.

To all these people, and all the people I did not mention, my heartfelt thank you.

I can't end without also mentioning the furry ones: Izzy, the snoring spaniel, and Abby, the joyful corgi. And finally, Budha, the krazy kitty, who contributed more than his share of typos to this book.

PART I

Availability

Without high availability, you have no reason to scale.

CHAPTER 1

What Is Availability?

No one cares if your system has great features if they can't use it.

One of the most important topics in architecting for scalable systems is availability. Although there are some companies and some services for which a certain amount of downtime is reasonable and expected, most businesses cannot have any downtime at all without it affecting their customer's satisfaction, and ultimately, the company's bottom line.

The following are fundamental questions that all companies must ask themselves when they determine how important system availability is to their company and their customers. It is these questions, and the inevitable answers to them, that are the core of why availability is critical to highly scaled applications:

- Why should someone buy your service if it is not operational when they need it?
- What do your customers think or feel when they need to use your service and it's not operational?
- How can you make your customers happy, make your company money, and meet your business promises and requirements, if your service is down?

Keeping your customers happy and engaged with your system is only possible if your system is operational. There is a direct and meaningful correlation between system availability and customer satisfaction.

High availability is such a critical component for building highly scalable systems that we will devote a significant amount of time to the topic in this book. How do you build a system (a service or application or environment) that is highly available even when a wide range of demands are placed it?

In this chapter, we'll define what availability is and how it compares to reliability. We use this in future chapters as we discuss the role availability plays in building highly scalable applications.

The Big Game

It's Sunday—the day of the big game. You've invited 20 of your closest friends over to watch the game on your new 300" Ultra Max TV. Everyone has come, your house is full of snacks and beer. Everyone is laughing. The game is about to start. And…

…the lights go out…

…the TV goes dark…

…the game, for you and your friends, is over.

Disappointed, you pick up the phone and call the local power company. The representative, unsympathetically, says: "We're sorry, but we only guarantee 95% availability of our power grid."

Why is availability important? Because your customers expect your service to work… all the time. Anything less than 100% availability can be catastrophic to your business.

Availability Versus Reliability

Availability and reliability are two similar but very different concepts. It is important to understand the difference between them.

Reliability, in our context, generally refers to the quality of a system. Typically, it means the ability of a system to consistently perform according to specifications. You speak of software as reliable if it passes its test suites, and does generally what you think it should do.

Availability, in our context, generally refers to the ability of your system to perform the tasks it is capable of doing. Is the system around? Is it operational? Is it responding? If the answer is "yes," it is available.

As you can see, availability and reliability are very similar. It is hard for a system to be available if it is not also reliable, and it is hard for a system to be reliable if it is not also available.

However, typically when we think about reliability and software, we are generally referring to the ability for software to perform what it is supposed to do. By and large, the main indicator of reliability is whether the software passes all of its test suites.

Moreover, when we think about availability, we think about whether the system is "up" and functional. If I send it a query, will it respond?

Here is what we mean when we use these terms:

Reliability
> The ability of your system to perform the operations it is intended to perform without making a mistake.

Availability
> The ability of your system to be operational when needed in order to perform those operations.

 A system that adds 2 + 3 and gets 6 has poor reliability. A system that adds 2 + 3 and never returns a result at all has poor availability. Reliability can often be fixed by testing. Availability is usually much harder to solve.

You can introduce a software bug in your application that can cause 2 + 3 to produce the answer 6. This can be easily caught and fixed in a test suite.

However, assume you have an application that *reliably* produces the result 2 + 3 = 5. Now imagine running this application on a computer that has a flaky network connection. The result? You run the application and sometimes it returns 5 and sometimes it doesn't return anything. The application may be *reliable*, but it is not *available*.

In this book, we focus almost exclusively on architecting highly *available* systems. We will assume your system is reliable, we will assume you know how to build and run test suites, and we will only discuss reliability when it has a direct impact on your system architecture or its availability.

What Causes Poor Availability?

What causes an application that previously performed well to begin exhibiting poor availability? There are many causes:

Resource exhaustion
> Increase the number of users or increase the amount of data in use in a system and your application may fall victim to resource exhaustion, resulting in a slower and unresponsive application.

Unplanned load-based changes
> Increases in the popularity of your application might require code and application changes to handle the increased load. These changes, often implemented quickly and at the last minute with little or no forethought or planning, increase the likelihood of problems occurring.

Increased number of moving parts

As an application gains popularity, it is often necessary to assign more and more developers, designers, testers, and other individuals to work on and maintain it. This larger number of individuals working on the application creates a large number of moving parts, whether those moving parts are new features, changed features, or just general application maintenance. The more individuals working on the application, the more moving parts within the application and the greater the chance for bad interactions to occur in it.

Outside dependencies

The more dependencies your application has on external resources, the more it is exposed to availability problems caused by those resources.

Technical debt

Increases in the applications complexity typically increases technical debt (i.e., the accumulation of desired software changes and pending bug fixes that typically build up over time as an application grows and matures). Technical debt increases the likelihood of a problem occurring.

All fast-growing applications have one, some, or all of these problems. As such, potential availability problems can begin occurring in applications that previously performed flawlessly. Often the problems will creep up on you; often they will start suddenly.

But most growing applications have the same problem. They eventually will begin having availability problems.

Availability problems cost you money, they cost your customer's money, and they cost you your customer's trust and loyalty. Your company cannot survive for long if you constantly have availability problems.

Building applications designed to scale means building applications designed for high availability.

CHAPTER 2

Five Focuses to Improve Application Availability

Building a scalable application that has high availability is not easy and does not come automatically. Problems can crop up in unexpected ways, that can cause your beautifully functioning application to stop working for all or some of your customers.

These availability problems often arise from the areas you least expect, and some of the most serious availability problems can originate from extremely benign sources.

A Simple Icon Failure

A classic example of the pitfalls of ignoring dependency failure occurred in a real-life application I worked on. The application provided a service to customers, and on the top of every page was a customizable icon representing the currently logged-in user. The icon was generated by a third-party system.

One day, the third-party system that generated the icon failed. Our application, which assumed that system would always work, didn't know what to do. As a result, our application failed as well. Our entire application failed simply because the icon-generation system—a very minor "feature"—failed.

How could we have avoided this problem? If we had simply anticipated that the third-party system might fail, we would have walked through this failure scenario during design and discovered that our application would fail subsequently. We could then have added logic to detect the failure and remove the icon if the failure occurred, or simply catch the error when it occurred and not allowed it to propagate down and affect the working aspects of the page.

A simple check and some error recovery logic would have kept the application operational. Instead, our application experienced a major site outage.

> All because of the lack of an icon.

No one can anticipate where problems will come from, and no amount of testing will find all issues. Many of these are systemic problems, not merely code problems.

To find these availability problems, we need to step back and take a systemic look at your application and how it works. Here are five things you can and should focus on when building a system to make sure that, as its use scales upwards, availability remains high:

- Build with failure in mind
- Always think about scaling
- Mitigate risk
- Monitor availability
- Respond to availability issues in a predictable and defined way

Let's look at each of these individually.

Focus #1: Build with Failure in Mind

As Werner Vogels, CTO of Amazon, says, "Everything fails all the time." Plan on your applications and services failing. It will happen. Now, deal with it.

Assuming your application will fail, how will it fail? As you build your system, consider availability concerns during all aspects of your system design and construction. For example:

Design

What design constructs and patterns have you considered or are you using that will help improve the availability of your software?

Using design constructs and patterns, such as simple error catching deep within your application, retry logic, and circuit breakers in a way that allows you to catch errors when they have affected the smallest available subset of functionality. This allows you to limit the scope of a problem and have your application still provide useful capabilities even if part of the application is failing.

Dependencies

What do you do when a component you depend on fails? How do you retry? What do you do if the problem is an unrecoverable (hard) failure, rather than a recoverable (soft) failure?

Circuit breaker patterns are particularly useful for handling dependency failures because they can reduce the impact a dependency failure has on your system.

Without a circuit breaker, you can decrease the performance of your application because of a dependency failure (for example, because an unacceptably long timeout is required to detect the failure). With a circuit breaker, you can "give up" and stop using a dependency until you are certain that dependency has recovered.

Customers

What do you do when a component that is a customer of your system behaves poorly? Can you handle excessive load on your system? Can you throttle excessive traffic? Can you handle garbage data passed in? What about excessive data?

Sometimes, denial-of-service attacks can come from "friendly" sources. For example, a customer of your application may see a sudden surge in activity that requires a significant increase in the volume of requests to your application. Alternatively, a bug in your customer's application may cause them to call your application at an unacceptably high rate. What do you do when this happens? Does the sudden increase in traffic bring your application down? Or can you detect this problem and throttle the request rate, limiting or removing the impact to your application?

Focus #2: Always Think About Scaling

Just because your application works now does not mean it will work tomorrow. Most web applications have increasing traffic patterns. A website that generates a certain amount of traffic today might generate significantly more traffic sooner than you anticipate. As you build your system, don't build it for today's traffic; build it for tomorrow's traffic.

Specifically, this might mean:

- Architect in the ability to increase the size and capacity of your databases.
- Think about what logical limits exist to your data scaling. What happens when your database tops out in its capabilities? Identify these and remove them before your usage approaches those limits.
- Build your application so that you can add additional application servers easily. This often involves being observant about where and how state is maintained, and how traffic is routed.[1]
- Redirect static traffic to offline providers. This allows your system to only deal with the dynamic traffic that it is designed to deal with. Using external content delivery networks (CDNs) not only can reduce the traffic your network has to

---

1 This topic is large enough for an entire chapter, even an entire book, of its own.

handle, but also allows the efficiencies of scale that CDNs provide in order to get that static content to your customers more quickly.

- Think about whether specific pieces of dynamic content can actually be generated statically. Often, content that appears dynamic is actually mostly static and the scalability of your application can be increased by making this content static. This "dynamic that can be static" data is sometimes hidden where you don't expect it, as the following tip discusses.

Is It Static or Is It Dynamic?

Often, content that seems dynamic is actually mostly static. Think about a typical top banner on a simple website. Frequently, this content is mostly static, but occasionally there is some dynamic content included in it.

For example, the top of the page might say "Log in" if you are not logged in, and say "Hello, Lee" if you are logged in (and, of course, assuming your name is Lee).

Does that mean the entire page must be generated dynamically? Not necessarily. With the exception of the login/greeting portion of the page, the page (or page portion) is static and can be easily provided by a CDN without any computation on your part.

When the majority of the banner is static, you can, in the user's browser, add the changeable content to the page dynamically (such as adding "Log In", or "Hello, Lee," as appropriate). By grouping this dynamic data together and processing it separately from the truly static data, you can increase the performance of your web page, and decrease the amount of dynamic work your application has to perform. This increases scalability, and ultimately, availability.

Focus #3: Mitigate Risk

Keeping a system highly available requires removing risk from the system. When a system fails, often the cause of the failure could have been identified as a risk before the failure actually occurred. Identifying risk is a key method of increasing availability. All systems have risk in them:

- There is risk that a server will crash
- There is risk that a database will become corrupted
- There is risk that a returned answer will be incorrect

- There is risk that a network connection will fail
- There is risk that a newly deployed piece of software will fail

Keeping a system available requires removing risk. But as systems become more and more complicated, this becomes less and less possible. Keeping a large system available is more about managing what your risk is, how much risk is acceptable, and what you can do to mitigate that risk.

We call this *risk management*. We will be talking extensively about risk management in Part II of this book. Risk management is at the heart of building highly available systems.

Part of risk management is *risk mitigation*. Risk mitigation is knowing what to do when a problem occurs in order to reduce the impact of the problem as much as possible. Mitigation is about making sure your application works as best and as completely as possible, even when services and resources fail. Risk mitigation requires thinking about the things that can go wrong, and putting a plan together, now, to be able to handle the situation when it does happen.

Example 2-1. Risk mitigation—the no-search web store

Imagine a web store that sells T-shirts. It's your typical online store that provides the ability to browse shirts on a home page, navigate to browse different categories of shirts, and search for a specific style or type of shirt.

To implement the search capability, a store such as this typically needs to invoke a separate search engine, which may be a separate service or may even be a third-party search provider.

However, because the search capability is an independent capability, there is risk to your application that the search service will not be able to function. Your risk management plan identifies this issue and lists "Failed Search Engine" as a risk to your application.

Without a risk mitigation plan, a failed search service might simply generate an error page or perhaps generate incorrect or invalid results—in either case, it is a bad customer experience.

A risk mitigation plan may say something like the following:

> We know that our most popular T-shirts are our red striped T-shirts, 60 percent of people who search our site end up looking at (and hopefully eventually buying) our famous red striped shirts. So, if our search service stops functioning, we will show an "I'm Sorry" page, followed by a list of our most popular T-shirts, including our red striped shirts. This will encourage customers who encounter this error page to continue to browse to shirts customers have historically found as interesting.

Additionally, we will show a "10% off next purchase" coupon, so that customers who can't find what they are looking for will be enticed to come back to our site in the future when our search service is functional again rather than looking elsewhere.

Example 2-1 demonstrates risk mitigation; the process of identifying the risk, determining what to do, and implementing these mitigations is risk management.

This process will often uncover unknown problems in your application that you will want to fix immediately instead of waiting for them to occur. It also can create processes and procedures to handle known failure modes so that the cost of that failure is reduced in duration or severity.

Availability and risk management go hand in hand. Building a highly available system is significantly about managing risk.

Focus #4: Monitor Availability

You can't know if there is a problem in your application unless you can see there is a problem. Make sure your application is properly instrumented so that you can see how the application is performing from an external perspective as well as internal monitoring.

Proper monitoring depends on the specifics of your application and needs, but usually entails some of the following capabilities:

Server monitoring
> To monitor the health of your servers and make sure they keep operating efficiently.

Configuration change monitoring
> To monitor your system configuration to identify if and when changes to your infrastructure impact your application.

Application performance monitoring
> To look inside your application and services to make sure they are operating as expected.

Synthetic testing
> To examine in real time how your application is functioning from the perspective of your users, in order to catch problems customers might see before they actually see them.

Alerting
> To inform appropriate personnel when a problem occurs so that it can be quickly and efficiently resolved, minimizing the impact to your customers.

There are many good monitoring systems available, both free and paid services. I personally recommend New Relic. It provides all of the aforementioned monitoring and alerting capabilities. As a Software as a Service (SaaS) offering, it can support the monitoring needs at pretty much any scale your application may require.[2]

After you have started monitoring your application and services, start looking for trends in your performance. When you have identified the trends, you can look for outliers and treat them as potential availability issues. You can use these outliers by having your monitoring tools send you an alert when they are identified, before your application fails. Additionally, you can track as your system grows and make sure your scalability plan will continue to work.

Establish internal private operational goals for service-to-service communications, and monitor them continuously. This way, when you see a performance or availability-related problem, you can quickly diagnose which service or system is responsible and address the problem Additionally, you can see "hot spots"—areas where your performance is not what it could be—and put development plans in place to address these issues.

Focus #5: Respond to Availability Issues in a Predictable and Defined Way

Monitoring systems are useless unless you are prepared to act on the issues that arise. This means being alerted when problems occur so that you can take action. Additionally, you should establish processes and procedures that your team can follow to help diagnose issues and easily fix common failure scenarios.

For example, if a service becomes unresponsive, you might have a set of remedies to try to make the service responsive. This might include tasks such as running a test to help diagnose where the problem is, restarting a daemon that is known to cause the service to become unresponsive, or rebooting a server if all else fails. Having standard processes in place for handling common failure scenarios will decrease the amount of time your system is unavailable. Additionally, they can provide useful follow-up diagnosis information to your engineering teams to help them deduce the root cause of common ailments.

When an alert is triggered for a service, the owners of that service must be the first ones alerted. They are, after all, the ones responsible for fixing any issues with their service. However, other teams who are closely connected to the troubled service and

---

2 I should point out that I work at New Relic, but this is not why I recommend it. I discovered and started using the New Relic tools before I started working there. My success in using its tools to solve my performance and availability problems is *why* I started working for New Relic, not the other way around.

---

depend on it might also want to be alerted of problems when they occur. For example, if a team makes use of a particular service, they may want to know when that service fails so that they can potentially be more proactive in keeping their systems active during the dependent service outage.

These standard processes and procedures should be part of a support manual available to all team members who handle oncall responsibility. This support manual should also contain contact lists for owners of related services and systems as well as contacts to call to escalate the problem if a simple solution is not possible.

All of these processes, procedures, and support manuals should be prepared ahead of time so that during an outage your oncall personnel know exactly what to do in various circumstances to restore operations quickly. These processes and procedures are especially useful because outages often occur during inconvenient times such as the middle of the night or on weekends—times when your oncall team might not perform at peak mental efficiency. These recommendations will assist your team in making smarter and safer moves toward restoring your system to operational status.

Being Prepared

No one can anticipate where and when availability issues will occur. But you can assume that they will occur, especially as your system scales to larger customer demands and more complex applications. Being prepared in advance to handle availability concerns is the best way to reduce the likelihood and severity of problems. The five techniques discussed in this chapter offer a solid strategy for keeping your applications highly available.

CHAPTER 3

Measuring Availability

Measuring availability is important to keeping your system highly available. Only by measuring availability can you understand how your application is performing now and examine how your application's availability changes over time.

The most widely held mechanism for measuring the availability of a web application is calculating the percent of time it's accessible for use by customers. We can describe this by using the following formula for a given period:

$$\text{Site availability percentage} = \frac{total\_seconds\_in\_period - seconds\_system\_is\_down}{total\_seconds\_in\_period}$$

Let's consider an example. Suppose that over the month of April, your website was down twice; the first time it was down for 37 minutes, and the second time it was down for 15 minutes. What is the availability of your website?

Example 3-1. Availability percentage

Total Number of Seconds Down $= (37 + 15) * 60 = 3,120\ seconds$

Total Number of Seconds in Month $= 30\ days * 86,400\ seconds/day = 2,592,000\ seconds$

$$\text{Site availability percentage} = \frac{total\_seconds\_in\_period - seconds\_system\_is\_down}{total\_seconds\_in\_period}$$

$$\text{Site availability percentage} = \frac{2,592,000\ seconds - 3,120\ seconds}{2,592,000\ seconds}$$

Site availability percentage = 99.8795

Your site availability is 99.8795%.

You can see from this example that it only takes a small amount of outage to have an impact on your availability percentage.

The Nines

Often you will hear availability described as "the nines." This is a shorthand way of indicating high availability percentages. Table 3-1 illustrates what it means.

Table 3-1. The Nines

Nines	Percentage	Monthly outage [a]
2 Nines	99%	432 minutes
3 Nines	99.9%	43 minutes
4 Nines	99.99%	4 minutes
5 Nines	99.999%	26 seconds
6 Nines	99.9999%	2.6 seconds

[a] This assumes a 30-day month with 43,200 minutes in the month.

In Example 3-1, we see that the website has fallen just short of the 3 nines metric (99.8795% compared to 99.9%). For a website that maintains 5 nines of availability, there can be only 26 *seconds* of downtime every *month*.

What's Reasonable?

What's a reasonable availability number in order to consider your system as high availability?

It is impossible to give a single answer to this question because it depends dramatically on your website, your customer expectations, your business needs, and your business expectations. You need to determine for yourself what number is required for your business.

Often, for basic web applications, 3 nines is considered *acceptable availability*. Using Table 3-1, this amounts to 43 minutes of downtime every month. For a web application to be considered highly available, often an indication of 5 nines is used. This amounts to only 26 *seconds* of downtime every month.

Don't Be Fooled

Don't be fooled into thinking your site is highly available when it isn't. Planned and regular maintenance that involves your application being unavailable still count against availability.

Here's a comment that I often overhear: "Our application never fails. That's because we regularly perform system maintenance. By scheduling weekly two-hour maintenance windows, and performing maintenace during these windows, we keep our availability high."

Does this group keep its application's availability high?

Let's find out.

Example 3-2. Maintenance Window Example Availability

$$\text{Site availability percentage} = \frac{total\_hours\_in\_period - hours\_system\_is\_down}{total\_hours\_in\_period}$$

$$hours\_in\_week = 7 \ days * 24 \ hours = 168 \ hours$$

$$hours\_unavailable\_each\_week = 2 \ hours$$

$$\text{Site availability (no failures)} = \frac{168 \ hours - 2 \ hours}{168 \ hours} = 98.8\%$$

$$\text{Site availability (no failures)} = 98.8\%$$

Without having a single failure of its application, the best this organization can achieve is 98.8% availability. This falls short of even 2 nines of availability (98.8% versus 99%).

Planned maintenance hurts nearly as much as unplanned outages. If your customer expects your application to be available and it isn't, your customer has a negative experience. It doesn't matter if you planned for the outage or not.

Availability by the Numbers

Measuring availability is important to keeping your system highly available, now and in the future. This chapter discussed a common mechanism for measuring availability and provided some guidelines on what is considered reasonable availability.

CHAPTER 4

Improving Your Availability When It Slips

Your application is operational and online. Your systems are in place, and your team is operating efficiently. Everything seems to be going well. Your traffic is steadily increasing and your sales organization is very happy. All is well.

Then there's a bit of a slip. Your system suffers an unanticipated outage. But that's OK; your availability has been fantastic until now. A little outage is no big deal. Your traffic is still increasing. Everyone shrugs it off—it was just "one of those things."

Then it happens again—another outage. Oops. Well, OK. Overall, we're still doing well. No need to panic; it was just another "one of those things."

Then another outage...

Now your CEO is a bit concerned. Customers are beginning to ask what's going on. Your sales team is starting to worry.

Then another outage...

Suddenly, your once stable and operational system is becoming less and less stable; your outages are getting more and more attention.

Now you've got real problems.

What happened? Keeping your system highly available is a daunting task. What do you do if availability begins to slip? What do you do if your application availability has fallen or begins to fall, and you need to improve it to keep your customers satisfied?

Knowing what you can do when your availability begins to slip will help you to avoid falling into a vicious cycle of problems. The following sections outline some steps you can take when your availability begins to falter.

Measure and Track Your Current Availability

To understand what is happening to your availability, you must first measure what your current availability is. By tracking when your application is available and when it isn't gives you an *availability percentage* that can show how you are performing over a specific period of time. You can use this to determine if your availability is improving or faltering.

You should continuously monitor your availability percentage and report the results on a regular basis. On top of this, overlay key events in your application, such as when you performed system changes and improvements. This way you can see whether there is a correlation over time between system events and availability issues. This can help you to identify risks to your availability.

 Refer back to Chapter 3 if you need a refresher on how to measure availability.

Next, you must understand how your application can be expected to perform from an availability standpoint. A tool that you can use to help manage your application availability is *service tiers*. These are simply labels associated with services that indicate how critical a service is to the operation of your business. This allows you and your teams to distinguish between mission-critical services and those that are valuable but not essential. We'll discuss service tiers in more depth in Chapter 16.

Finally, create and maintain a *risk matrix*. With this tool, you can gain visibility into the technical debt and associated risk present in your application. Risk matrices are covered more fully in Chapter 7 and risk in general is discussed in Chapters 5 and 6.

Now that you have a way to track your availability and a way of identifying and managing your risk, you will want to review your risk management plans on a regular basis.

Additionally, you should create and implement mitigation plans to reduce your application risks. This will give you a concrete set of tasks you and your development teams can implement to tackle the riskiest parts of your application. This is discussed in detail in Chapter 8.

Automate Your Manual Processes

To maintain high availability, you need to remove unknowns and variables. Performing manual operations is a common way to insert variable results and/or unknown results into your system.

You should never perform a manual operation on a production system.

When you make a change to your system, the change might improve or it might compromise your system. Using only repeatable tasks gives you the following:

- The ability to test a task before implementing it. Testing what happens when you make a specific change is critical to avoiding mistakes that cause outages.

- The ability to tweak the task to perform exactly what you want the task to do. This lets you implement improvements to the change you are about to make, before you make them.

- The ability to have the task reviewed by a third party. This increases the likelihood that the task will not have unexpected side effects.

- The ability to put the task under version control. Version control systems allow you to determine when the task is changed, by who, and for what reasons.

- The ability to apply the task to related resources. Making a change to a single server that improves how that server works is great. Being able to apply the same change to every affected server in a consistent way makes the task even more useful.

- The ability to have all related resources act consistently. If you continuously make "one off" changes to resources such as servers, the servers will begin to *drift* and act differently from one another. This makes it difficult to diagnose problematic servers because there will be no baseline of operational expectation that you can use for comparison.

- The ability to implement repeatable tasks. Repeatable tasks are auditable tasks. Auditable tasks are tasks that you can analyze later for their impact, positive or negative, on the system as a whole.

There are many systems for which no one has access to the production environment. Period. The only access to production is through automated processes and procedures. The owners of these systems lock down their environments like this specifically for the aforementioned reasons.

In summary, if you can't repeat a task, it isn't a useful task. There are many places where adding repeatability to changes will help keep your system and application stable. This includes server configuration changes, performance tuning tweaks and adjustments, restarting servers, restarting jobs and tasks, changing routing rules, and upgrading and deploying software packages.

Automated Deploys

By automating deploys, you guarantee changes are applied consistently throughout your system, and that you can apply similar changes later with known results. Additionally, rollbacks to known good states become more reliable with automated deployment systems.

Configuration Management

Rather than "tweaking a configuration variable" in the kernel of a server, use a process to apply the change in an automated manner. For example, write a script that will make the change, and then check that script into your software change management system. This enables you to make the same change to all servers in your system uniformly. Additionally, when you need to add new servers to your system or replace old ones, having a known configuration that can be applied improves the likelihood that you can add the new server to your system safely, with minimal impact. Tools like Puppet and Chef can help make this process easier to manage.

The same applies to all infrastructure components, not just servers. This includes switches, routers, network components, and monitoring applications and systems.

For configuration management to be useful, it must be used for *all* system changes, *all* the time. It is *never* acceptable to bypass the configuration management system to make a change under any circumstances. Ever.

Don't Worry, I Fixed It

You would be surprised the number of times I have received an operational update email that said something like: "We had a problem with one of our servers last night. We hit a limit to the maximum number of open files the server could handle. So I tweaked the kernel variable and increased the maximum number of open files, and the server is operational again."

That is, it is operating correctly until someone accidentally overwrites the change because there was no documentation of the change. Or, until one of the other servers running the application has the same problem, but did not have this change applied.

Consistency, repeatability, and unfaltering attention to detail is critical to make a configuration management process work. And a standard and repeatable configuration management process such as we describe here is critical to keeping your scaled system highly available.

Change Experiments and High Frequency Changes

Another advantage of having a highly repeatable, highly automated process for making changes and upgrades to your system is that it allows you to experiment with changes. Suppose that you have a configuration change you want to make to your servers that you believe will improve their performance in your application (such as the maximum number of open files change described in "Don't Worry, I Fixed It" on page 22). By using an automated change management process, you can do the following:

- Document your proposed change.
- Review the change with people who are knowledgeable and might be able to provide suggestions and improvements.
- Test the change on servers in a test or staging environment.
- Deploy your change quickly and easily.
- Examine the results quickly. If the change didn't have the desired results, you can quickly roll back to a known good state.

The keys to implementing this process are to have an automated change process with rollback capabilities, and to have the ability to make small changes to your system easily and often.[1] The former lets you make changes consistently, the latter lets you experiment and roll back failed experiments with little to no impact on your customers.

Automated Change Sanity Testing

By having an automated change and deploy process,[2] you can implement an automated sanity test of all changes. You can use a browser testing application for web applications or use something such as New Relic Synthetics to simulate customer interaction with your application.

When you are ready to deploy a change to production, you can have your deployment system first automatically deploy the change to a test or staging environment. You can then have these automated tests run and validate that the changes did not break your application.

If and when those tests pass, you can automatically deploy the change in a consistent manner to your production environment. Depending on how your tests are constructed, you should be able to run the tests regularly on your production environment, as well, to validate that no changes break anything there.

By making the entire process automated, you can increase your confidence that a change will not have a negative impact on your production systems.

---

1 According to Werner Vogels, CTO of Amazon, in 2014 Amazon did 50 million deploys to individual hosts. That's about one every second.

2 This could be, but does not need to be a modern continuous integration and continuous deploy (CI/CD) process.

Improve Your Systems

Now that you have a system to monitor availability, a way to track risk and mitigations in your system, and a way to easily and safely apply consistent changes to your system, you can focus your efforts on improving the availability of your application itself.

Regularly review your risk matrix (discussed earlier in this chapter and in Chapter 7) and your recovery plans. Make reviewing them part of your postmortem process. Execute projects that are designed to mitigate the risks identified in your matrix. Roll out those changes in an automated and safe way, using the sanity tests discussed earlier. Examine how the mitigation has improved your avaiability. Continue the process until your availability reaches the level you want and need it to be.

You can learn about how to recover from failing services in Chapter 13.

Publish availability metrics to your management chain. This visibility will help with justifying projects such as these to improve your system availability.

Your Changing and Growing Application

As your system grows, you'll need to handle larger and larger traffic and data demands. This increase in traffic and data can cause availability issues to compound. Part IV provides extensive coverage of application scaling, and many of the topics discussed in that part will help in improving an application that is experiencing availability issues. In particular, managing mistakes and errors at scale is discussed in Chapter 14. Service-level agreement (SLA) management is discussed in Chapter 18. Service tiers, which you can use to identify key availability-impacting services, are discussed in Chapters 16 and 17.

Implement Game Day testing, which measures how your application performs in various failure modes. This is discussed further in Chapter 9.

Keeping on Top of Availability

Typically, your application will change continuously. As such, your risks, mitigations, contingencies, and recovery plans need to constantly change.

Knowing what you can do when your availability begins to slip will help you to avoid falling into a vicious cycle of problems. The ideas in this chapter will help you manage your application and your team to avoid this cycle and keep your availability high.

PART II

Risk Management

You cannot possibly manage the risk in your system if you cannot identify the risk in your system.

> ...but there are also unknown unknowns—the ones we don't know we don't know. And if one looks throughout the history of our country and other free countries, it is the latter category that tend to be the difficult ones.
>
> —Donald Rumsfeld

CHAPTER 5

What Is Risk Management?

All complex systems have risk. It is an inevitable part of all systems. It is impossible to remove all risk from a complex system such as a web application. However, examining your risk and determining how much risk is acceptable is important in keeping your system healthy.

This chapter, provides an overview of what risk is and how we can identify it. It then introduces a process called *risk management*, which helps us to reduce the effect of risk on our applications.

Let's now take a look at Example 5-1, which revisits the big game example from Chapter 1.

Example 5-1. Risk management of the big game

Here's a brief synopsis of the big game example we looked at earlier: it's Sunday—the day of the big game. You've invited friends over to watch it on your new TV. The game is about to start. And…the lights go out and the TV goes dark. The game, for you and your friends is over. You call the power company, and they say "We're sorry, but we only guarantee 95% availability of our power grid."

The power company in this example is taking a risk. They are risking that the power won't go off during a big game.

They even have it quantified (95% likely power will stay on).

The power company knows the types of things that can cause power to go out, such as a power line breaking. As such, to ensure power lines won't break, they will typically:

- Bury them (to protect them from wind)
- Harden them (to reduce the chance a wind storm can blow it down)
- Put in redundant power systems (so one keeps working even if another is down)

But these strategies have a cost. Is it worthwhile investing in hardened power lines? Is it worth the cost to bury them? Is the cost of the risk worth the investment in reducing the risk? These types of questions are risk management questions, and these are the types of questions we will consider in this chapter.

Managing Risk

Risk management involves determining where the risk is within your system, determining which risks must be removed and which remain, and then mitigating the remaining risks to reduce their likelihood and severity.

When a risk *triggers* (or *occurs*), you or your system suffer a loss. This loss can be data lost by your company or a customer. It can be a lack of availability in your application by your customers. The loss can be invalid or erroneous results. Ultimately, any of these can result in your customers losing trust in your ability to manage their data and their business. This, ultimately, will cost you money.

However, you must weigh this loss against a competing aspect: what is the cost of removing the risk to prevent it from happening?

Ultimately, risk management is balancing the cost of removing a risk with the cost of having the risk occur.

Identify Risk

Your first step in managing risk is creating a list of all known risks, along with their severity and their likelihood of occurring.

We call this list a *risk matrix*, an example of which is shown in Figure 5-1.

Figure 5-1. Example risk matrix

Creating the matrix initially involves brainstorming. You can get ideas for what to put in your risk matrix from multiple sources:

- Collective wisdom of the developers
- Known high-support areas
- Known threat vectors or vulnerabilities
- Known areas where the system is incomplete or missing capabilities
- Known poor performance areas
- Known traffic spikes and patterns
- Specific concerns from business owners, support personnel, or users
- Known technical debt in your system

You will likely find that there are obvious entries in the list, but there should also be entries that surprise you. This is good. You want to uncover as many of your risk vulnerabilities as possible, and if some of them don't come as a surprise to you, you probably haven't dug deep enough.

Creating the risk matrix involves assigning prioritized values for the likelihood of the risk occurring and the impact (severity) of the problem caused if the risk does occur.

We will discuss this list extensively in Chapter 7.

Remove Worst Offenders

After compiling your initial list, review it and identify the risk entries that are your worst unmitigated offenders. How do you know which risks are the worst offenders? Look for risks that occur often or risks that haven't occurred yet but would cause serious problems to your system if they did. The absolute worst offenders are risks that are highly likely to occur or occur often *and* cause serious harm to your system. Chapter 6 discusses the difference between severity and likelihood, and how to use this information to help manage your risks. This information will help you find your worst offenders.

In Figure 5-1, an example risk that might be one of our worst offenders is "Frontend fails if user identity service is down."

Once you've identified a few of the top offenders, add items to your roadmap to make sure these are addressed in a timely manner.

Mitigate

For all risks, whether they are the worst offenders or not, brainstorm if there are things you can do that will either reduce the frequency or likelihood of the risk occurring, or reduce the severity of the problem if the risk does occur. These things are called *risk mitigators*.

Risk mitigators can be highly valuable. You are especially looking for mitigators that will reduce the risk (either severity or likelihood or both) yet are simple or inexpensive to implement.

Let's take a look at the risk "Frontend fails if user identity service is down" shown in Figure 5-1. For this risk, a potential mitigation to consider is to cache user identity information so that some information may be available for the frontend to use, even if the user identity service is down.

You can focus on your worst offenders, finding ways to reduce the severity of those risks. But also look at risks that you might not be able to fix any time soon. Finding mitigations to these risks which reduce the severity or likelihood can be nearly as valuable as fixing the risk altogether.

Review Regularly

The risk matrix can quickly become stale if you don't review it regularly. You should review your risk matrix as a team at least quarterly, but perhaps monthly for very active and highly critical systems. Additionally, review it after each incident. Was the incident properly covered by a known risk?

When you review the matrix, first look for new risks that have been recently introduced or newly identified. Add new entries for these risks. Also, remove old entries for items that are no longer risks.

Then look for severity or likelihood changes. Often, mitigations were helpful and managed to reduce the severity or likelihood. Or, more knowledge has come forward that makes a risk either more likely to occur or perhaps more severe. This is frequently the case if a risk actually triggered since your last review; you might feel that a risk marked as a low likelihood that actually did occur should perhaps be restated as a risk with a higher likelihood. Now, are there risks that you can remove (fix) by putting them on your roadmap?

Finally, look for new or updated mitigations that you can put into play.

Managing Risk Summary

How do you manage risk in your systems? There are some basic steps to follow to accomplish it:

Identify risk
    First, make a list of all your known risks in your system; this list is called a risk matrix. Prioritize the list.

Remove worst offenders

Find the biggest offenders in the list, and put a plan together to tackle them.

Mitigate

For the major risk items that you cannot remove, put together a mitigation plan to reduce the severity or likelihood of the risk from occurring.

Review regularly

Review your risk matrix regularly.

CHAPTER 6

Likelihood Versus Severity

It is important to understand the relationship between severity and likelihood. Managing risk involves knowing when you need to be concerned about severity and not likelihood, or vice versa. Understanding the difference is essential in analyzing the seriousness of risks to your system.

We treat all risks as being composed of two components:

Severity
> The cost if the risk happens (for example, what is the impact if customers don't have power?).

Likelihood
> The chance of the risk happening (for example, how likely is a big windstorm?).

Managing risks is managing these two values. You can reduce the severity of a risk happening or you can reduce the likelihood. For any given risk, you don't need to do both. But considering both is important to understanding the best path forward in managing risks.

 The significance of a risk is the combination of the severity of the risk happening with the likelihood of it happening. To successfully manage risk, you must consider both of these values and how they relate to each other. To reduce risk, you need to reduce at least one of these two values for any given risk.

The best way to understand the difference is by looking at examples of various risks and how their likelihood and severity differ. We'll use the following example through the remainder of this chapter to help explain the differences:

Let's assume that we are managing an online T-shirt store. This store is your typical online retailer. They provide a listing of T-shirts available, individual pages that show the details of each T-shirt, including pictures of what they look like, and an order processing system that customers can use to purchase and pay for T-shirts that they want shipped to them.

Now let's look at some example risks for this store.

The Top 10 List: Low Likelihood, Low Severity Risk

Using our T-shirt store example, let's assume that the site has a feature that appears on the upper-right side that shows the top 10 best-selling T-shirts. Visitors on the site can see these best sellers and then click to go to and purchase one of them quickly and easily.

Now, what happens if the top 10 list can't be generated for some reason (perhaps due to a service failure)? If it can't be displayed, let's instead assume a static list of T-shirts is displayed, but those shirts displayed aren't necessarily the current top 10 best sellers. This service failure doesn't happen often, because the top 10 list is easy to generate and doesn't tend to have any problems.

What is the risk to our store for having a top 10 list displayed?

Let's look at this risk:

- The *likelihood* of the risk is low because the service that displays the list is apparently quite reliable (I stated the list is easy to generate).
- But if the list does not appear, how severe is the problem? I stated that if the top 10 list doesn't appear, an alternate list is shown. Although not ideal, the impact on our customers is probably quite low, and the impact on our business would likely not be very large, either. As such, the *severity* of this risk is also low.
- This risk is a Low/Low Risk. This means it has a low likelihood and a low severity.

Risks like this are easy to ignore and typically do not need further attention, because they are rare events and the events themselves have very little negative impact.

The Order Database: Low Likelihood, High Severity Risk

Using our T-shirt store example, let's assume that your list of orders is stored in a typical database. Whenever a customer generates an order, an entry is created in the database. As you process, collect payment, and ship these orders, you update the data in the database. Later, the data is used to generate financial reports that you can use to show how much business you are doing for purposes such as business planning and tax calculations.

Because the database is important, you run it on high-quality hardware with replicated system components (such as a RAID disk array). You also do regular backups of the data.

However, the database is still a single point of failure. The database contains significant amounts of business-critical data, and your website can't function (you can't even take any orders) if the database is not available. Losing the database would be a big loss.

What is the risk to our store associated with the order processing system's database?

Let's look at this risk:

- The *likelihood* of the failure is quite low, because you are using high-quality, replicated hardware for the database. The database is quite reliable.

- However, the *severity* of a failure in the database would be quite high. This is because if the database does fail, your entire order-processing pipeline will be down, and you risk losing business-critical data.

- This risk is a Low/High Risk. This means it has a low likelihood and a high severity.

- Risks like this are easy to miss because they do not happen very often (likelihood is low). However, they can be very expensive risks if they are ignored because the cost of failure is very high.

Given the high *severity*, this is a risk that you might want to look at mitigating that severity. For example, you might want to have a hot database replica standing by, so that you can quickly flip from the broken database to the hot replica. This will let you continue working without significant loss of time or data. Alternatively, you might want to switch to a database technology that distributes data across multiple servers so that you can continue to function even if one of your database servers fail.

Using one of these techniques might very well turn this risk from a Low/High Risk back down to a Low/Medium Risk (low likelihood, medium severity) or even a Low/Low Risk (low likelihood, low severity).

Mitigations such as this, which can dramatically reduce the severity of a problem, are discussed further in Chapter 8.

Custom Fonts: High Likelihood, Low Severity Risk

Using our T-shirt store example, suppose that you decide to spruce up your site a bit by using custom fonts in all of your text and descriptions. You've found the perfect font to use, and it is provided (and hosted) by a third-party font service provider. To use the font, your customer's web browser downloads it directly from the third-party service provider. If the custom font is not available, a standard system font is used and the page looks like it did previously.

However, you've noticed this font service provider has problems on occasion, much more often than you'd want. When this service provider has a problem, your customers can't use the beautiful custom font.

This happens a lot, unfortunately.

What is the risk to your store of using the beautiful custom font?

Let's look at this risk:

- The *likelihood* of the font not appearing is high, because the service provider is inconsistent and has problems often.
- However, when the problem does occur, your site continues to work—it just doesn't look quite as spruced up as you'd like. Hence, the *severity* of the problem is low.
- Your site might be missing some of its glitz, but it is fully functional without significant problems.
- This risk is a High/Low Risk. This means it has a high likelihood of occurring but has a low severity.

Mitigations for this risk involve reducing the *likelihood* of the problem occurring. You can reduce the likelihood of this problem occurring by working with the third-party provider to improve the availability of the service. Or, you can compile a list of backup providers that offer the same or similar fonts, and switch to them if the first provider doesn't work. These are ways you can reduce the *likelihood* of the problem occurring.

There is not much you can do to reduce the severity, given that it is already quite low.

T-Shirt Photos: High Likelihood, High Severity Risk

Using our T-shirt store example, let's look at the T-shirt images (pictures) that appear on your site. These are an incredibly important part of your store because people are typically not going to buy T-shirts if they can't see what they look like. If your T-shirt images do not appear, your customers will leave your site and you'll lose orders.

However, the server on which you are hosting your images is flaky. It goes in and out of service and seems to be having problems reading images from its disk. The server is old and needs to be replaced. It fails often and needs to be rebooted regularly. It goes out of service for parts replacement constantly. Yet, this is the server used to host your images.

What is the risk of your site becoming unusable because the images are not available?

Let's look at this risk:

- The *likelihood* of the images not displaying is high because the server is flaky and fails often.
- The *severity* of this risk is also high, because if the images aren't available, your customers will go away and not place orders.
- This risk is a High/High Risk. This means it has a high likelihood of occurring (the hardware fails often) *and* it has a high severity when it does occur (customers won't buy from you).

These types of risks are the most scary. This is a risk that is highly likely to happen, and the problem it introduces is serious to your business.

These are the risks to which you should pay the most attention.

This example might seem obvious, but there likely are many such High/High Risks in your applications. Often, though, these risks might not be obvious until you look closely at your system. This is why risk management is so important.

CHAPTER 7

The Risk Matrix

The first step in managing risk is understanding the risk that is already in your system. Identifying, labeling, and prioritizing your known risks is what the *risk matrix* is all about.

First introduced in Chapter 5, the risk matrix is a critical aspect of managing the risk in your system. It is a table that contains a living view of the state of all the known risk in your system.

Figure 7-1 contains an example risk matrix.

Figure 7-1. Example risk matrix

Each row in the matrix represents a single, quantifiable risk that is present in your system. The columns in the spreadsheet contain the details of that specific risk item.

For each risk item the following information is kept:

Risk ID

This is a unique identifier assigned to the risk. It can be anything, but a unique integer identifier is usually the easiest and is sufficient.[1]

System

This is the name of the system, subsystem, or module that contains the risk. This information is dependent on the specifics of your application, but it could be things like "FrontEnd," "PrimaryDb," "ServiceA," or similar.

Owner

The name of an individual (or team) who owns this risk and is responsible for mitigation plans and resolution plans.

Risk description

This is a summary description of the risk. It should be short enough to be easily scanned and recognized yet long enough to uniquely and accurately identify the risk.

Date identified

The date the risk was identified and added to the matrix.

Likelihood

This identifies the likelihood (low, medium, or high) of the risk occurring. This value is discussed in greater detail in Chapter 6. You will use this value to sort your risk matrix to determine which ones to be the most concerned with and which ones require the most immediate attention.[2]

Severity

This is the severity or impact (low, medium, or high) of the risk occurring. This value is discussed in greater detail in Chapter 6. You will use this value to sort your risk matrix to determine which ones to be the most concerned with and which ones require the most immediate attention.

Mitigation plan

This column provides a description of any migitations that can be used, or are being used, to reduce the severity or likelihood of this risk.

---

1 The ID should *not* be the row number in the spreadsheet, however. This is because the rows in the matrix will likely be sorted and new ones added and removed, thus changing the spreadsheet row number for a risk. The Risk ID should be an identifier that does not change for the life of the tracking of the risk.

2 To ease column sorting by the Likelihood and Severity values, you might want to make them numeric, 1–3 for Low to High, or some other way. A common sorting trick is to use "1-Low," "2-Medium," "3-High," and then use your spreadsheet program's capabilities to restrict the values allowed to just these three.

Status

This column indicates what the status of the risk is. This is typically something like "active," "mitigated," "fix in progress," or "resolved."

ETA

This is the estimated time for when the final resolution for this risk is planned (if known).

Monitoring

This column indicates whether you are monitoring for this risk to occur, and if so, the steps you've taken to accomplish this. If you are not monitoring the risk, you should indicate why and estimate a date for when you will be able to do so.

Triggered plan

If this risk does occur, what is your plan for dealing with it? The triggered plan is usually a management-level plan rather than an incident-response plan.[3]

Comment

Use this column for any other information about this risk that doesn't fit or doesn't belong in the risk description.

Additionally, other values that are important to your organization can be added as you see fit. For example:

Tracking ID

If you have a bug tracking or roadmap tracking system that contains an entry for this risk, you can put the bug or roadmap tracking ID number in this field.

History

Has this risk already triggered in the past? When? How often?

Scope of the Risk Matrix

At this point, you're probably wondering "Should I have one risk matrix for the entire company, or one for each team or service?"

This is a good question. One matrix for the entire company is fine for a small company, but it can quickly become unwieldy. One per service affords good visibility at the service level, but reduced visibility at the company level. Questions such as "which service has the most significant risk to the company?" become hard to answer.

I recommend one risk matrix per team. Because decision making on what features or issues to work on and their priority is often handled at the team level, it makes sense

---

3 Incident response plans should be readily available to your oncall personnel in your incident playbook or other tools.

for the risk matrix to be managed and prioritized at the team level. You can find more information about team level management in Chapter 15.

Bottom line, you should scope your risk matrices as makes sense for your organization. As such, one risk matrix should be used for each team, group, or organization that typically manages its own decisions about work scoping and prioritization. They may receive input and guidance from upper management, but most work is prioritized and executed at this organizational level.

Creating the Risk Matrix

First, begin with one of the risk matrix templates. We have created some for you in the most popular spreadsheet programs. They are available for download on our website (*http://bit.ly/architectbookdl*). Although you are free to customize it as needed, for your first risk matrix, you should stick as closely as possible to this template. After you have some experience using the matrix and managing risks, you can customize as you see fit.

The template has an example risk on it to demonstrate how you might use it. Feel free to delete that before continuing.

Figure 7-2. Downloaded risk matrix template

Brainstorming the List

When you have your template ready, your first step is to brainstorm a list of the risks you feel should be included. Try to include any risk you can think of, not just those with which you are concerned. Don't analyze them during this process—just brain dump all that you can think of.

There are several good sources of insights for this brainstorm:

Dev team
> Have a meeting with your development team. The team members will have an amazingly large number of worries on their mind about their services. Listen to their concerns, and add risk items for each one that comes up.

Support

Look at your support volume. Are there areas where you are seeing a higher than normal support load? What do your support people say? Do you have support forums you can review? High support areas are a common source of system risks.

Threat vectors

Think about known threat vectors and security vulnerabilities. Each of these, no matter how big or how important, is a risk to your service.

Feature backlog

Go through your feature backlog. Are there capabilities of your system that are missing that are critical to the health of your system? Look especially for monitoring and maintenance-related backlog items.

Performance

Think about the performance of your system. Are there areas you are aware of that have poor performance?

Business owners

Talk to your business owners. What concerns do they have?

Extended team

Talk to your extended team, including internal users, dependent teams, Q/A staff, and so on. What concerns do they have?

Systems and processes

Do you have documented systems and processes in place? Are there places where necessary documentation for how your application functions is missing, or perhaps is held only in the heads of a few individuals?

Technical debt

Do you have known, specific technical debt in your system? Examples of technical debt include areas of code that are hard to understand or are more complicated or have more moving pieces than are necessary. Areas of known technical debt are almost always risk items.

You will likely find that there are obvious entries in the list, but there should also be entries that surprise you. This is good. You want to uncover as many of your risk vulnerabilities as possible, and if none of them come as a surprise to you, you probably haven't dug deep enough.

Set the Likelihood and Severity Fields

Now, go through the list and set the likelihood and severity field for each item. Use Low/Medium/High (or similar variation) values for each of the two fields.

Make sure to keep the concepts of likelihood and severity distinct in your mind. Refer to Chapter 6 if necessary. It is often very easy to confuse them as you are working on this step.

It might be helpful to go through and set likelihood first, and then go back and set severity for each item. Remember, it's quite normal for a risk item to be very severe if it occurs, but almost impossible to occur (or, alternatively, very common to occur but not very important if it does occur). You will end up with items in all combinations of H/H, H/L, L/H, and L/L state. This is normal and expected.

However you decide to do this task, you will not end up with a meaningful list if you confuse these two values.

Another brainstorming session with your development team is a great way to accomplish this task. This should be a distinct brainstorming session from the aforementioned session, which identifies the risks. Don't label them at the same time that you identify them.

Risk Item Details

Now, fill in the other basic details of the risk matrix. This includes things like System, Owner, Date Identified, and Status.

Make sure to assign a risk ID to each item (a simple numbering from 1…n is reasonable).

Are you monitoring for this risk? Indicate in the Monitoring field whether you have the ability to be notified if this risk is triggered.

Mitigation Plan

Starting with the highest severity items first, begin to put together mitigation plans for each item. Then move on to the highest likelihood items.

A *mitigation plan* is a plan for how you are going to, *now or in the near future*, put in changes that are designed to either reduce the severity of the risk or reduce the likelihood. A mitigation plan is not designed to *remove* the risk—instead, it simply reduces the severity or likelihood.

After you perform the steps indicated in the mitigation plan, it will be expected that the severity or likelihood will reduce, and this mitigation plan will be removed. A new mitigation plan can be introduced, if appropriate.

You do not need a mitigation plan for every item in the matrix. There might be items that clearly must be fixed and cannot be mitigated. Additionally, Low Likelihood/Low Severity items do not need to be mitigated.

Triggered Plan

A *triggered plan* is a plan for what you are going to do *if the risk actually occurs*. This can be something as simple as "fix the bug," but it can also be more elaborate. For instance, if a risk occurs, are there tasks you can take right then that will reduce the impact? If so, they should be elaborated as part of the triggered plan.

Starting with the items with the highest severity first, begin to put together trigger plans for each item.

 Note that the triggered plan should not be seen as a replacement for incident-response documentation, such as playbooks. The risk matrix should *not* be a tool that must be consulted during an incident response. Instead, the matrix (including the triggered plan) should be a tool used by management to determine follow-up actions for the risk occurring.

Using the Risk Matrix for Planning

After your risk matrix is created, it should be consulted during all planning sessions. This includes long-range planning sessions with product management, but also SCRUM-level planning sessions with your engineers.

During every planning session, the most critical risks[4] should be examined. The following questions should be asked:

- Is this risk worse now than the last time I examined it?
- Should we schedule work during this planning period to remove (fix) risks in our system?
- Should we schedule work during this planning period to mitigate risks in our system, and hence reduce their likelihood or severity?

Every planning session should include a review of the risk matrix, and items on the risk matrix (either fixing risks or mitigating risks) should be included in your work prioritization process.

If your team makes use of a tool such as Jira or Pivotal Tracker during your planning sessions, you might want to add items in your tracking tool for the most critical risks. If you do that, you should refer to the Risk ID of the corresponding risk in your

---

4 The most critical risks are those risks with the highest likelihood, the highest severity, or especially items for which both likelihood and severity are high.

tracking tool item, and also add a Tracking ID column to your risk matrix to store the ID of the item from your tracking tool.

Maintaining the Risk Matrix

The biggest challenge with the risk matrix is that it is very easy for the matrix to become stale. Your natural tendency is to create the matrix, and then put it into a drawer and forget about it.

If you do not take time to maintain your risk matrix, it will rapidly become out of date and useless.

To keep your risk matrix up to date and accurate, you should schedule regular reviews of the matrix with the appropriate stakeholders, including your development team and partners. This can be monthly, but it should not be any less often than quarterly. The exact recurrence cycle depends on your business processes. If you have a planning cycle starting soon, performing a regular review of the matrix before that process begins is ideal.

Risk Matrix Review Attendees

Note that it is useful to change your risk matrix reviewers regularly. By requiring different individuals to review and comment on your risk matrix, you'll get a fresh perspective and the review will be less likely to turn into a "same old rut" type of meeting.

During this review, you need to:

Look for new risks
> Have there been new risks added to your system or recently identified? Make sure these are captured on the risk matrix.[5]

Remove old risks
> Are there risks on the matrix that no longer apply—either because they can't occur anymore or because the underlying cause has been fixed? If so, remove these.

Update likelihood and severity
> Look for likelihood and severity changes. Often, recently implemented mitigations were helpful in reducing the likelihood or severity, or additional informa-

---

5 However, we recommend that the moment you believe you have identified a new risk, you add it to the matrix. Don't wait for a review session. You can wait for the review session to update all the data in the risk, but you should document it immediately once discovered.

tion has been gathered that will warrant a change in the likelihood or severity status. Make these updates.

Review top risks

Review all the risks that are either high likelihood or high severity (or both). Discuss these specific risks individually and make sure all the information is correct for them. Are there new or updated mitigation plans that can be put in place? What about triggered plans? Are you monitoring the risk? If not, why not? What else can you do to improve your situation with these risks?

Review less critical risks

Keep going down the likelihood and severity curve, looking at less critical risks as time permits. You do not have to review every risk every time, but make sure the top risks are all looked at often. In addition, you might want to schedule a session to examine in detail the less critical risks, just so they don't get ignored and to make sure there aren't hidden or missed reasons why they should be ranked higher on your list.

Sharing Your Risk Matrix with Management

You should share your risk matrix with your product management and upper management teams. This can be an effective tool in communicating issues with those not directly involved day to day with your team, and keeping specific issues on the minds of those that need to know them.

One idea I saw implemented recently occurred before a management offsite meeting. Someone was identified to take all the risk matrices for the entire company and combine them into one giant list for the offsite (a read-only copy). Then, only the high likelihood or high severity items were kept; the rest were deleted. This master "High/ High" list was then used during the management offsite as a way for discussing overall company risk with their products, as well as a way to level set expectations of what types of things different teams put into their matrices, and learn best practices.

CHAPTER 8

Risk Mitigation

The mitigation column in the risk matrix is used to show what mitigations can be, or are being used to reduce the severity, the likelihood, or both values for a given risk. It is all about taking a High/High risk[1] and changing it to a High/Medium risk or a Medium/High risk.[2] It is not about *fixing* the risk, only mitigating the severity or likelihood of the risk.

As described in "Mitigation Plan" on page 44, there is a basic process that you can follow for mitigating risks. A *mitigation plan* details the steps you are going to take (either immediately or in the near future) in order to reduce the likelihood or severity of the risk.

Risk mitigation is knowing what to do when a problem occurs so that you can reduce the impact of the problem as much as possible. Mitigation is about making sure your application works as best and completely as possible, even when services and resources fail.

Let's look at an example of a mitigation plan. Let's assume that we have a database that is used for an application, such as the one described in Chapter 5. Let's further assume that we already run the database on high-quality hardware with replicated components, such as using a RAID disk array, and server-grade redundant hardware. We believe our database is highly stable and highly available. On our risk matrix, we have the risk of a database failure as having a Low likelihood.

---

1 See Chapter 6 for a full description of severity, likelihood, the definition of High/High, and so on.

2 Or lower any other combination, such as Medium/High to Medium/Medium, or Medium/Low to Low/Low.

However, the database is still a single point of failure. If the database server fails (unlikely though that is), your entire system goes out of service. On our risk matrix, we would list this as a High severity.

This risk is a Low/High risk, and is very similar to the risk described in "The Order Database: Low Likelihood, High Severity Risk" on page 34.

What can we do to mitigate this risk? Well, one idea is to add multiple active database read replicates, and have them available on hot standby, as shown in Figure 8-1. If our main database server ever fails, having an active database standby ready to go will dramatically reduce the amount of time your system is down while the problem is being fixed. This reduces the severity of the risk, perhaps even making it a Low/Medium risk.

This is a mitigation plan.

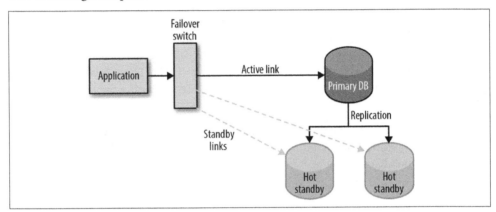

Figure 8-1. Example database hot standby for risk mitigation

What's the difference between risk mitigation and risk management? They are similar but different concepts:

Risk mitigation
> Risk migitation is about reducing the impact of a risk by either reducing the likelihood that the risk will occur, or reducing the severity of the problem if the risk does occur.

Risk management
> Risk management is understanding the play between removing risk and mitigating risk. It's knowing whether it is prudent, timely, and cost effective to remove a risk or simply reduce the impact of the risk.

Recovery Plans

If a known risk does occur, you must deal with the consequences. You can use a *recovery plan* to create a known set of actions to take to deal with those consequences and repair the problem that the risk introduced. Recovery plans typically do not impact the likelihood, just the severity of a risk.

A recovery plan is a particular type of risk mitigation that specifically involves reducing the severity of the risk when it does occur. A recovery plan describes what you do if a known risk happens. A recovery plan can describe the following:

- Actions to take to stop the problem as quickly as possible.
- Actions to take to implement a workaround to reduce the impact of the problem.
- Messages to inform customers of what the problem is and what they can do to reduce the impact on them.
- Escalation processes to use and people within the company to inform about the problem. This lets all parts of the company understand and deal with the problem and any fallout.

A good recovery plan is constructed in advance, as part of the risk mitigation plan for a given risk, so that when a problem does occur (a risk is triggered) everyone knows what needs to happen to recover from the problem.

The recovery plan should contain:

- Details of what must be happening that would trigger the recovery plan to be implemented.
- The list of actors that need to be involved in implementing the recovery plan.
- Step-by-step instructions for implementing the recovery plan, and which actor should execute those steps.
- Management, escalation, and notifications that need to be informed.
- Required follow-up that must happen after the problem is resolved.

The recovery plan should be stored in a well-known location to your team—that is, a place where everyone on your team will know to go during a crisis situation. This could be in a support book or an internal support intranet. After a recovery plan is executed, a postmortem of the problem should occur and the recovery plan should be analyzed to determine if any improvements or changes are warranted.

The simple existence of a valid recovery plan for a specific risk item is an example of a valid *risk mitigation* plan that you can use to reduce the severity of a given risk.

Recovery Plan

The replication process described in Figure 8-1 is the beginning of a recovery plan for the risk of catastrophic database failure. However, to be a complete recovery plan, you would also need to include a process for implementing failover, criteria for determining when the failover can occur, an approval process for implementing the failover, and postmortem cleanup after the failover.

Disaster Recovery Plans

A *disaster recovery plan* is an example of a recovery plan that is designed to describe what the company should do if a specific type of disaster hits the company. These types of disasters tend to have a severity of High but will typically have a likelihood of Low.

An example of a disaster that warrants a disaster plan is the loss of one or more data centers for your application (whether that is caused by technical issues, a natural disaster, or by a significant security breach).

You can create and manage disaster recovery plans just like recovery plans. The only real difference between a disaster recovery plan and a typical recovery plan is the seriousness of the risk they are mitigating and potentially the level of detail and involvement in implementing the plan.

Typically, disaster recovery plans have significantly more visibility within the company and the management and ownership of the company. There may be preestablished, business-specified recovery times required for these types of disasters. But this does not effectively distinguish them from recovery plans.

Improving Our Risk Situation

Risk mitigation is an important process in improving the availability and scalability of our applications by reducing the impact that risk plays in our application. It is a recognition that although removing a risk might not be possible or practical, reducing its impact or severity might very well be possible, and often is sufficient to give us the desired level of application health we desire.

When used in conjunction with a risk matrix, risk mitigation plans provide a useful tool to improve the health of your application.

CHAPTER 9

Game Days

A habit that is easy yet dangerous to fall into is to build recovery plans and disaster plans, and then shove them in a drawer and ignore them until they are needed.

If you do that, it is almost guaranteed that by the time you need the recovery/disaster plans, they will be incorrect or out of date. In addition, if you do not keep them up to date, you open up the possibility for a number of other problems to be introduced, making the plans impossible or impractical to implement successfully.

As such, you should plan to test your recovery/disaster plans on a regular basis. It should become part of your company culture to regularly test these plans and other risk mitigations.

One model for testing these plans is to run *Game Days*. A Game Day is when you test invoking a specific failure mode into your system and watch to see how your operators and engineers respond to it, including how they implement any recovery/disaster plans. After the Game Day, a postmortem review will uncover changes and issues with your plans that need to be made. These changes will keep your plans fresh and updated, and ready to be used when a real problem occurs.

Staging Versus Production Environments

You might be wondering whether you should test recovery plans on a staging environment or on your live production application. This is a tough question and it does not have a simple answer. Let's take a closer look at each of these options:

Staging/test environments
> Testing recovery plans in a staging/test environment is the safest option. Using a staging or test environment allows you to perform invasive testing that would normally disrupt production environments in inappropriate ways. In addition,

you can perform those tests without fear of mistakes that could cause production outages. If you decide to use a staging/test environment to test your recovery plan, keep the following information in mind:

- Make sure the staging/test environment is completely independent from your production environment. The environment should not depend on any production resources, and the production resources should not depend on any resources from the testing environment. See Figure 9-1.

- Make sure the staging and test environment mimics your production environment as closely as possible. Using a staging/testing environment to test your recovery plan can be effective, and you can use these types of environments for testing a wide variety of destructive failure scenarios. However, they cannot guarantee the same results that would occur in a production system. This is because production systems are almost always scaled to more and larger servers, contain a larger data set, and manage significantly more traffic in real time. These differences make certain types of testing in non-production environments unuseful. Ideally, the test environment should be scaled to the same size as your production environment and be seeded with the same data used in your production environment; however, this is usually not financially viable and can be difficult logistically. If you believe your testing requires a system scaled to the same level as your production environment, you might want to consider production environment testing instead.

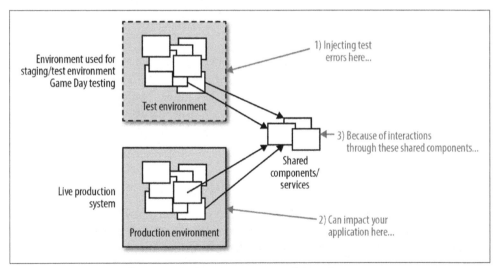

Figure 9-1. Dangers of not separating environments for testing

Production environments

Testing risk and recovery plans in a production environment seems illogical. Why would you force a failure mode in production just to make sure that your production systems don't fail? The answer is simple: if you test recovery on your production environment at a time when your team is available and sharp (in other words, not in the middle of the night) and at a time of day that has the least impact on your customers, and carefully consider the steps your tests will take, you can safely perform testing on your production environments under real-world situations and get valuable data on how your efforts would really perform in real failure conditions.

If you decide to use a production environment to test your recovery plan, keep the following information in mind:

- Be aware of the impact of your injected failure on your live customers.
- Consider the business aspects of the testing. What's the trade-off between adding additional production risk to your customers' use of the system, versus the reduced long-term risk of learning from the results of those tests?
- Perform the tests at a time when your staff members are at their sharpest (during the workday, when your staff is normally in the office), but also at a time that will minimize impact to your customers (such as at potentially slower traffic times, and not during critical time periods like end-of-month or end-of-quarter sales pushes).
- Make sure you have the processes in place that can implement necessary fixes, and roll back failed fixes, quickly and easily.

Concerns with Running Game Days in Production

Game Days on your production environment should be planned and monitored very carefully. Planned appropriately, a production Game Day can be quite revealing of problems within your production environment. Here are some example production Game Days that you could run:

Server failing

What happens if a single server in your system fails? Try taking one out of service. If your system has a proper amount of redundancy built in, this should not have any impact on your production system. But use the removal as a test of your systems to detect such a problem, and your recovery plan for replacing the lost server.

Network partition

What happens if a network outage or partition occurs? Planned carefully, you can simulate a network partition without significantly endangering your production application. But they can be a solid test for the notification and follow-through actions of your system and your teams in responding to the event.

Data center failure

What happens if an entire data center goes down? Planned carefully, your application should be able to handle such an event. How do you respond to such an outage?

Random failures

What happens if you introduce smaller, random errors into your system? Does your application recover from these errors reasonably?

The last item in this list in many ways feels the most threatening. Why? Because you can imagine what will happen when a server goes down or a data center goes down. You probably already have plans in place for dealing with that (if you don't, then you should). But a "random" problem, even if only small in scale, feels like something out of control. Well, it is. But it is these random events that cause you the most problems in building highly available, risk mitigated systems.

Chaos Monkey

Netflix takes the random failures problem to a new level. The company has a system called *Chaos Monkey* built into its application. This system randomly and regularly introduces random faults into the application, *in the production environment*, with *live running customers*. Exactly what Chaos Monkey does and how it does it are not known to the engineers and operators managing the application. Instead, it is assumed that engineers have put the proper recovery and mitigation processes in place so that the problems that Chaos Monkey introduces can be resolved or worked around without affecting customers at all.

Chaos Monkey only runs during business hours when engineers are around and available to respond to any problems that don't self-correct. The philosophy around Chaos Monkey is to encourage, and actually *require*, the building of highly available, self-reliant services and applications that can survive and recover without human intervention. This is tested during the day when humans are around, with the hope that the problems won't occur at night when the application is busier (more customers) and engineers must be paged into work. It is a novel approach that works well for Netflix.

Chaos Monkey is a great example of a best practice for Game Day testing, and Netflix has done some miraculous things with its Game Day infrastructure. However, it took significant effort, significant resources, and a significant commitment before Netflix could get to the point where running Chaos Monkey in production could be done in a safe and effective way. Chaos Monkey should not be your first step into production

---

Game Day testing. But it can be a reasonable goal to work toward if your company has the commitment to make it happen.

Game Day Testing

Game Day testing is an important avenue of testing that can help assure your production environment will operate fully at a systemic level. It allows validating your support plans and processes in a safe manner so that when you really need to use them, they will work without issue.

Done properly, Game Day testing can dramatically improve your system availability at scale and reduce your risk of serious problems or failures in your production environment.

CHAPTER 10

Building Systems with Reduced Risk

In Chapter 8, we learned how to mitigate risks that exist within your system and applications. However, there are things you can do to proactively build your applications with a reduced risk profile. This chapter reviews a few of these techniques. This is far from an exhaustive list, but it should at least get you thinking about risk reduction as you build and grow your applications.

Redundancy

Building in redundancy is an obvious step to improving the availability and reliability of your application. This inherently reduces your risk profile as well. However, redundancy can add complexity to an application, which can increase the risk to your application. So, it is important to control the complexity of the additional redundancy to actually have a measurable improvement to your risk profile.

Here are some examples of "safe" redundancy improvements:

- Design your application so that it can safely run on multiple independent hardware components simultaneously (such as parallel servers or redundant data centers).

- Design your application so that you can run tasks independently. This can help recovery from failed resources without necessarily adding significantly to the complexity of the application.

- Design your application so that you can run tasks asynchronously. This makes it possible for tasks to be queued and executed later, without impacting the main application processing.

- Localize state into specific areas. This can reduce the need for state management in other parts of your application. This reduction in the need for state management improves your ability to utilize redundant components.

- Utilize *idempotent interfaces* wherever possible. Idempotent interfaces are interfaces that can be called repeatedly in order to assure an action has taken place, without the need to worry about the implications of the action being executed more than once. Idempotent interfaces facilitate error recovery by using simple retry mechanisms.

Examples of Idempotent Interfaces

Using the example of a car that has an interface to control how fast it goes, the following would be an example of an idempotent interface:

- Set my current speed to 35 miles per hour

Whereas the following would be an example of a nonidempotent interface:

- Increase my current speed by 5 miles per hour

The idempotent interfaces can be called multiple times, and only the first call has an effect. Successive or duplicate calls make no change to the speed of the car. Telling the car to go 35 miles per hour repeatedly has no effect over telling it just once. However, nonidempotent interfaces have an impact on the speed of the car each time they are called. Telling a car to increase speed by 5 miles per hour repeatedly will result in a car that is continuously going faster and faster.

With an idempotent interface, a "driver" of this automated car has to tell the car only how fast it should be going. If, for some reason, it believes the request to go 35 miles per hour did not make it to the car, it can simply (and safely) resend the request until it is sure the car received it. The driver can then be assured that the car is, in fact, going 35 miles per hour.

With a nonidempotent interface, if a "driver" of the car wants the car to go 35 miles per hour, it sends a series of commands instructing the car to accelerate until it's going 35 miles per hour. If one or more of those commands fails to make it to the car, the driver needs some other mechanism to determine the speed of the car and decide whether to reissue an "increase speed" command. It cannot simply retry an increase speed command—it must figure out whether it needs to send the command. This is a substantially more complicated (and error-prone) operation.

Using idempotent interfaces lets the driver perform simpler operations that are less error prone than using a nonidempotent interface.

Redundancy Improvements That Increase Complexity

What are some examples of redundancy improvements that increase complexity? In fact, there are many that might seem useful, but their added complexity can cause more harm than good, at least for most applications.

Consider the example of building a parallel implementation of a system. This way if one of them fails, the other one can be used to implement the necessary features. Although this might be necessary for some applications for which extreme high availability is important (such as the space shuttle), it often is overkill and results in increased complexity, as well. Increased complexity means increased risk.

Another example is overtly separated activities. Microservices are a great model to impove the quality of your application and hence reduce risk. Chapter 12 contains more information on using services and microservices. However, if taken to an extreme, building your systems into too finely decomposed microservices can result in an overall increase in application complexity, which increases risk.

Independence

Multiple components utilizing shared capabilities or components may present themselves as independent components, but in fact, they are all dependent on a common compontent, as shown in Figure 10-1.

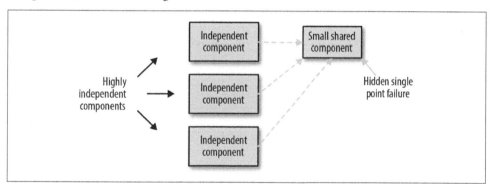

Figure 10-1. Dependency on shared components reduces independence

If these shared components are small or unknown, they can inject single point failures into your system.

Consider an application that is running on five independent servers. You are using five servers to increase availability and reduce the risk of a single server failure causing your application to become unavailable. Figure 10-2 shows this application.

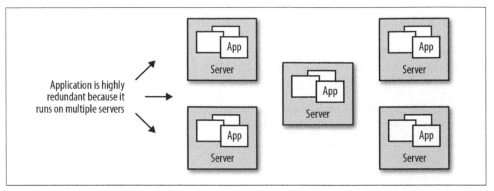

Figure 10-2. Independent servers…

But what happens if those five servers are actually five virtual servers all running on the same hardware server? Or if those servers are running in a single rack? What happens if the power supply to the rack fails? What happens if the shared hardware server fails?

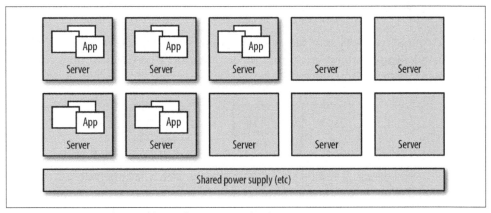

Figure 10-3. …aren't as independent as you think

Your "independent servers" might not be as independent as you think.

Security

Bad actors have always been a problem in software systems. Security and security monitoring has always been a part of building systems, even before large-scale web applications came about.

However, web applications have become larger and more complicated, storing larger quantities of data and handling larger quantities of traffic. Combined with a higher usefulness to the data available within these applications, this has led to a huge increase in the number of bad actors attempting to compromise our applications. Compromises by bad actors can be directed at acquiring highly sensitive private data, or they can be directed at bringing down large applications and making them unavailable. Some bad actors do this for monetary gain, while others are simply in it for the thrill. Whatever the motivation, whatever the result, bad actors are becoming a bigger problem.

Web application security is well beyond the purview of this book.[1] However, implementing high-quality security is imperative to both high availability and mitigating risk of highly scaled applications. The point here is that you should include security aspects of your application in your risk analysis and mitigation, as well as your application development process. However, the specifics of what that includes are beyond the scope of this book.

Simplicity

Complexity is the enemy of stability. The more complex a system becomes, the less stable it is. The less stable, the riskier it becomes and the lower the availability it is likely to have.

Although our applications are becoming larger and significantly more complicated, keeping simplicity in the forefront as you architect and build your application is critical to keep the application maintainable, secure, and low risk.

One common place where modern software construction principles tend to increase complexity more than perhaps is necessary is in microservice-based architectures. Microservice-based architectures reduce the complexity of individual components substantially, making it possible for the individual services to be easily understood and built using simpler techniques and designs. However, although they reduce the complexity of the individual microservice, they increase the number of independent modules (microservices) necessary to build a large-scale application. By having a larger number of independent modules working together, you increase the interdependence on the modules, and increase the overall complexity of the application.

It is important as you build your microservice-based application that you manage the trade-off between simpler individual services and more complex overall system design.

---

1 O'Reilly has many titles available about security and web security.

Self-Repair

Building self-righting and self-repairing processes into our applications can reduce the risk of availability outages.

As discussed in Chapter 3, if you strive for 5 nines of availability, you can afford no more than 26 seconds of downtime every month. Even if you only strive for 3 nines of availability, you can afford only 43 minutes of downtime every month. If a failure of a service requires someone to be paged in the middle of the night to find, diagnose, and fix the problem, those 43 minutes are eaten up very quickly. A single outage can result in missing your monthly 3 nines goal. And to maintain 4 nines or 5 nines, you have to be able to fix problems without any human intervention at all.

This is where self-repairing systems come into play. Self-repairing systems sound like high-end, complex systems, but they don't have to be. A self-repairing system can be nothing more than including a load balancer in front of several servers that reroutes a request quickly to a new server if the original server handling a request fails. This is a self-repairing system.

There are many levels of self-repairing systems, ranging from simple to complex. Here are a few examples:

- A load balancer that reroutes traffic to a new server when a previous server fails.
- A "hot standby" database that is kept up to date with the main production database. If the main production database fails or goes offline for any reason, the hot standby automatically picks up the "master" role and begins processing requests.
- A service that retries a request if it gets an error, anticipating that perhaps the original request suffered a transient problem and that the new request will succeed.
- A queuing system that keeps track of pending work so that if a request fails, it can be rescheduled to a new worker later, increasing the likelihood of its completion and avoiding the likelihood of losing track of the work.
- A background process (for example, something like Netflix's Chaos Monkey) goes around and introduces faults into the system, and the system is checked to make sure it recovers correctly on its own.
- A service that requests multiple, independently developed and managed services to perform the same calculation. If the results from all services are the same, the result is used. If one (or more) independent service returns a different result than the majority, that result is thrown away and the faulty service is shut down for repairs.

These are just some examples. Note that the more involved systems at the end of the list also add much more complexity to the system. Be careful of this. Use self-repairing systems where you can to provide significant improvement in risk reduction for a minimal cost in complexity. But avoid complicated systems and architectures designed at self-repair that provide a level of reliability higher than you really require, at the cost of increasing the risk and failures that the self-repair system itself can introduce.

Operational Processes

Humans are involved in our software systems, and humans make mistakes. By using solid operational processes, you can minimize the impact of humans in your system, and reducing access by humans to areas where their interaction is not required will reduce the likelihood of mistakes happening.

Use documented, repeatable processes to reduce one significant aspect of the human involvement problem—human forgetfulness: forgetting steps, executing steps out of order, or making a mistake in the execution of a step.

But documented repeatable processes only reduce that one significant aspect to the human involvement problem. Humans can introduce other problems. Humans make mistakes, they "fat finger" the keyboard, they think they know what they are doing when they really don't. They perform unrepeatable actions. They perform unauditable actions. They can perform bad actions in emotional states.

The more you can automate the processes that humans normally perform in your production systems, the fewer mistakes that can be introduced, and the higher the likelihood that the tasks will work.

Rebooting a Server

Suppose that you regularly reboot a server (or series of servers) for a specific purpose (we won't provide commentary on whether this is a good idea operationally).

You could simply have the user log in to the server, become superuser, and execute the "reboot" command. However, this introduces several problems:

- You now have to give the ability to log in to your production servers to anyone who might need to perform that command. Further, they must have superuser permission to execute the reboot command.

- While someone is logged in as superuser to the server, they could accidentally execute another command, one that causes the server to fail.

- While someone is logged in as superuser to the server, they could act as a bad actor and execute something that would intentionally bring harm to the server, such as running rm-rf / on Linux.

- You will likely have no record that the action occurred, and no record of who did the reboot and why.

Instead of using the manual process to reboot the server, you could implement an automated process that performs the reboot. In addition to doing the reboot, it could provide the following benefits:

- It would reduce the need to give login credentials to your production servers, eliminating both the likelihood of mistakes as well as of bad actors doing bad things.
- It could log all actions taken to perform the reboot.
- It could log who requested the reboot.
- It could validate that the person who requested the reboot has permissions to do the reboot (fine-grained permissions—you could grant access to reboot the server to a group of people without giving them any additional access rights).
- It could make sure that any other necessary actions occur before the server is rebooted. For instance, temporarily remove the server from the load balancer, shut down the running applications gracefully, and so on.

You can see that by automating this process, you avoid mistakes and you give the ability to have more control over who and how the operation is performed.

PART III

Services and Microservices

A service is a distinct enclosed system that provides business functionality in support of building one or more larger products.

CHAPTER 11

Why Use Services?

Traditionally, applications appear as single, large, distinct monoliths. The single monolith encompasses *all* business activities for a single application. To implement an improved piece of business functionality, an individual developer must make changes within the single application, and all developers making changes must make them within the same single application. Developers can easily step on one another's toes, and make conflicting changes that result in problems and outages.

In a service-oriented architecture, individual services are created that encompass a specific subset of business logic. These individual services are interconnected to provide the entire set of business logic for the application.

The Monolith Application

Figure 11-1 shows an application that is a large, single entity with a complex, indecipherable infrastructure.

This is how most applications begin to look if they are constructed and grow as monolithic applications. In Figure 11-1, you see there are five independent development teams working on overlapping areas of the application. It is impossible to know who is working on what piece of the application at any point in time, and code-change collisions and problems are easy to imagine. Code quality and hence application quality and availability suffer. Additionally, it becomes more and more difficult for individual development teams to make changes without having to deal with the effect of other teams, incompatible changes, and a molasses effect to the organization as a whole.

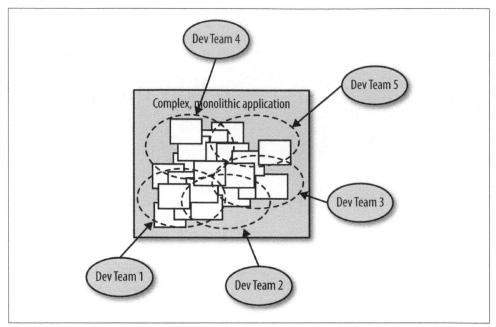

Figure 11-1. A large, complex, monolithic application

The Service-Based Application

Figure 11-2 presents the same application constructed as a series of services.

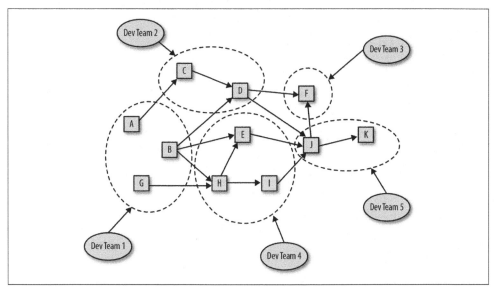

Figure 11-2. A large, complex, service-based application

Each service has a clear owner, and each team has a clear, nonoverlapping set of responsibilities.

Service-oriented architectures provide the ability to split an application into distinct domains that are each managed by individual groups within your organization. They enable the separation of responsibilities that are critical for building highly scaled applications, allowing work to be done independently on individual services without affecting the work of developers in other groups working on the same overall application.

When building highly scaled applications, service-based applications provide the following benefits:

Scaling decisions
> This makes it possible for scaling decisions to be made at a more granular level, which fosters more efficient system optimization and organization.

Team assignment and focus
> This lets you assign capabilities to individual teams in such a way that teams can focus on the specific scaling and availability requirements of their system in-the-small and have confidence that their decisions will have the appropriate impact at the larger scale.

Complexity localization
> Using service-based architectures, you can think about services as black boxes, making it so that only the owners of the service need to understand the complexity within that service. Other developers need only know what capabilities your service provides, without knowing anything about how it works internally. This compartmenting of knowledge and complexity facilitates the creation of larger applications and lets you manage them effectively.

Testing
> Service-based architectures are easier to test than monolithic applications, which increases your reliability.

> Service-oriented architectures can, however, increase the complexity of your system as a whole if the service boundaries are not designed properly. This complexity can lead to lower scalability and decreased system availability. So, picking appropriate service and service boundaries is critical.

The Ownership Benefit

Let's take a look at a pair of services.

In Figure 11-3, we see two services owned by two distinct teams. The Left Service is consuming the capabilities exposed by the Right Service.

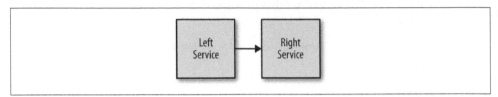

Figure 11-3. A pair of services

Let's look at this diagram from the perspective of the Left Service owner. Obviously, that team needs to know the entire structure, complexity, connectedness, interactions, code, and so on for their service. But what does it need to know about the Right Service? As a start, the team needs to know the following:

- The capabilities provided by the service.
- How to call those capabilities (the API syntax).
- The meanings and results of calling those capabilities (the API semantics).

That's the *basic* information that the Left Service team needs to know. What don't they need to know about the Right Service? Lots of things, for example:

- They do not need to know whether the Right Service is a single service, or a construction of many subservices.
- They do not need to know what services the Right Service depends on to perform its responsibilities.
- They do not need to know what language(s) the Right Service is written in.
- They do not need to know what hardware or system infrastructure is needed to operate the Right Service.
- They do not even need to know *who* is operating the Right Service (however, they do need to know how to contact the owner in case there are issues with it).

The Right Service can be as complex or simple as needed, as shown in Figure 11-4. But to the owners of the Left Service, the Right Service can be thought of as nothing more than a black box, as shown in Figure 11-5. As long as they know what the interface to the box is (the API), they can use the capabilities the black box provides.

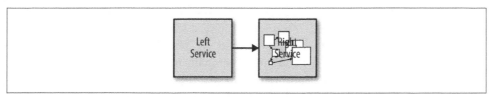

Figure 11-4. What's inside the Right Service

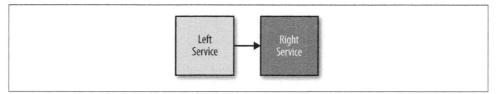

Figure 11-5. Right Service complexity hidden from dependencies

To manage this, the Left Service must be able to depend on a *contract* that the Right Service provides. This contract describes everything the Left Service needs to use the Right Service.

The contract contains two parts:

The capabilities of the service (the API)
- What the service does
- How to call it and what each call means

The responsiveness of the service
- How often can the API be used?
- When can it be used?
- How fast will the API respond?
- Is the API dependable?

All of this information describes the contract that the owners of the Right Service provide to the Left Service describing how the Right Service operates. As long as the Right Service behaves to this contract, the Left Service doesn't have to know or care anything about how the Right Service performs those commitments.

The last part of the contract, the *responsiveness* part, is called a *service-level agreement*, or *SLA*. It is a critical component in allowing the Left Service to depend on the Right Service without knowing anything about how the Right Service works.

We discuss SLAs in great detail in Chapter 18.

By having a clear ownership for each service, teams can focus on only those portions of the system for which they are responsible, along with the *API contracts* provided by the service owners of the services they depend on. This separation of responsibility makes it easier to scale your organization to contain many more teams; because the coupling between the teams is substantially looser, it doesn't matter as much how far away (organizationally or physically) one team is from another. As long as the contracts are maintained, you can scale your organization as needed to build larger and more complicated applications.

The Scaling Benefit

Different parts of your application have different scaling needs. The component that generates the home page of your application will be used much more often than the component that generates the user settings page.

By using services with clear APIs and API contracts between them, you can determine and implement the scaling needs required for each service independently. This means that if your home page is the most frequently called page, you can provide more hardware to run that service than the service that manages your user settings page.

By managing the scaling needs of each service independently, you can do the following:

- Provide more accurate scaling by having the team that owns the specific capability involved closely in the scaling decision.
- Save system resources by not scaling one component simply because another component requires it.
- Provide ownership of scaling decisions back to the team that knows the most about the needs of the service (the service owner).

CHAPTER 12

Using Microservices

A service provides some capabilities that are needed by the rest of the application. Example include billing services (which offer the component that bills customers), account creation services (which manage the component that creates accounts), and notification services (which include functionality for notifying users of events and conditions).

A service is a standalone component. The word "standalone" is critical. Services meet the following criteria:

Maintains its own code base
> A service has its own code base that is distinct from the rest of your code base.

Manages its own data
> A service that requires maintaining state has its own data that is stored in its own datastore. The only access to this separated data is via the service's defined API. No other service may directly touch another service's data or state information.

Provides capabilities to others
> A service has a well-defined set of capabilities and it provides these capabilities to other services in your application. In other words, it provides an API.

Consumes capabilities from others
> A service uses a well-defined set of capabilities provided by others and uses them in a standard, supported manner. In other words, it uses other service's APIs.

Single owner
> A service is owned and maintained by a single development team within your organization. A single team may own and maintain more than one service, but a single service can have only a single team that owns and maintains it.

What Should Be a Service?

How do you decide when a piece of an application or system should be separated out into its own service?

This is a good question, and one that does not have a single correct answer. Some companies that "service-ize" split their application into many (hundreds or thousands) of very tiny microservices. Others split their application into only a handful of larger services. There is no right answer to this problem. However, the industry is trending toward smaller microservices, and more of them. Technologies such as Docker have made these larger number of microservices a viable system topology.

We use the term *services* and *microservices* interchangeably in this book.

Dividing into Services

So, how do you decide where service boundaries should be? Company organization, culture, and the type of application can play a major role in determining service boundaries.

Following are a set of guidelines that you can use to determine where service boundaries can be. These are guidelines, not rules, and they are likely to change and morph over time as our industry progresses. They are useful to help individuals begin thinking about services and think about what should be a service.

Here at a high level are the guidelines (in order of priority):

Specific business requirements
> Are there any specific business requirements (such as accounting, security, or regulatory) that drive where a service boundary should be?

Distinct and separable team ownership
> Is the team that owns the functionality distinct and separable (such as in another city, or another floor, or even just a different manager) that will help specify where a boundary should be?

Naturally separable data
> Is the data it manages naturally separable from other data used in the system? Does putting data in a separate datastore overly burden the system?

Shared capabilities/data
> Does it provide some shared capabilities used by lots of other services and does that shared capability require shared data?

Let's now look at these each individually and figure out what they mean.

Guideline #1: Specific Business Requirements

In some cases, there will be specific business requirements that dictate where a service boundary should be. These might be regulatory, legal, security, or some critical business need.

Example 12-1. Payment processing

Imagine your system accepts online credit card payments from your customers. How should you collect, process, and store these credit cards and the payments they represent?

A good business strategy would be to put the credit card processing in a different service, separate from the rest of the system.

Putting critical business logic such as credit card processing into its own service is valuable for several reasons:

Legal/regulatory requirements
> There are legal and regulatory requirements around how you store credit cards that require you to treat them in different ways from other business logic and other business data. Separating this into a distinct service makes it easier to treat this data differently from the rest of your business data.

Security
> You might need additional firewalls for security reasons around these servers.

Validation
> You might need to perform additional production testing to verify security of these capabilities in ways significantly stronger than other parts of your system.

Restricting access
> You will typically want to restrict access to these servers so that only necessary personnel have access to highly sensitive payment information such as credit cards. You typically do not want or need to provide access to these systems to your entire engineering organization.

Guideline #2: Distinct and Separable Team Ownership

Applications are becoming more and more complicated, and typically larger groups of developers are working on them, often with more specialized responsibilities. Coordination between teams becomes substantially harder as the number of developers, the number of teams, and the number of development locations grow.

Services are a way to give ownership of smaller, distinct, separable modules to different teams.

General Guideline

A single service should be owned and operated by a single team that is typically no larger than three to eight developers. That team should be responsible for all aspects of that service.

By doing this, you loosen up the interteam dependencies and make it much easier for individual teams to operate and innovate independently from one another.

Team Ownership

As previously stated, a single service should be owned and operated by a single team, but a single team can own and operate more than one service. The key is to make sure that all aspects of a single service are under the influence of a single team. This means that team is responsible for all development, testing, deployment, performance, and availability aspects of that service.

However, that one team can have the ability to successfully manage more than one service, depending on the complexity and activity involved in those services. Additionally, if several services are very similar in nature, it might be easier for a single team to manage all those services.

A team can own or manage more than one service, but a service should be owned and managed by only one team.

Separate team for security reasons

Sometimes, you want to restrict the number and scope of individuals who have access to the code and data stored within a given service. This is especially true for services that have regulatory or legal constraints (as discussed in Example 12-1). Limiting access to a service with sensitive data can decrease your exposure to issues involved in the compromising of that data. In cases like this, you might physically limit access to the code, the data, and the systems hosting the service to only the key personnel required to support that service.

Additionally, splitting related sensitive data into two or more services, each owned by distinct teams, can reduce the chances of that data being compromised by making it less likely that multiple services with distinct owners will all have data compromised.

Example 12-2. Splitting data for security reasons

In Example 12-1, the credit card numbers themselves can be stored in one service. The secondary information necessary to use those credit cards (such as billing address and CCV code) could be stored in a second service. By splitting this information across two services, each owned and operated by individual teams, you limit the

---

chance that any one employee can inadvertently or intentionally expose enough data for a rogue agent to use one of your customer's credit cards inappropriately.

You might even choose to not store the credit card numbers in your services at all and instead store them in a third-party credit card processing company's services. This ensures that, even if one of your services is compromised, the credit cards themselves will not be.

Guideline #3: Naturally Separable Data

One of the requirements for a service is that its managed state and data needs to be separate from other data. For a variety of reasons, it is problematic to have multiple independent code bases both operating on the same set of data. Separating the code and the ownership is only effective if you also separate the data.

Figure 12-1 shows a service (Service A) that is trying to access data stored in another service (Service B). It illustrates the correct way for Service A to access data stored in Service B, which is for Service A to make an API call to Service B, and then let Service B access the data in its database itself.

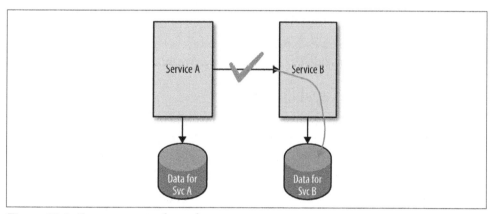

Figure 12-1. Correct way to share data

If instead, Service A tries to access the data for Service B directly, without going through Service B's API, as is shown in Figure 12-2, all sorts of problems can occur. This sort of data integration would require tighter coordination between Service A and Service B than is desired, and it can cause problems when data maintenance and schema migration activities need to occur. In general, the accessing of Service B's data directly by Service A without involving Service B's business logic in that process can cause serious data versioning and data corruption issues. It should be strictly avoided.

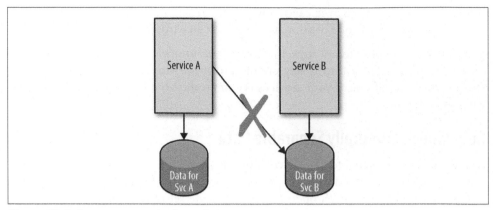

Figure 12-2. Incorrect way to share data

As you can see, determining data division lines is an important characteristic in determining service division lines. Does it make sense for a given service to be the "owner" of its data and provide access to that data only via external service interfaces? If the answer is "yes," this is a good candidate for a service boundary. If the answer is "no," it is not a good service boundary.

A service that needs to operate on data owned by another service must do so via published interfaces (APIs) provided by the service that owns that data.

Guideline #4: Shared Capabilities/Data

Sometimes a service can be created simply because it is responsible for a set of capabilities and its data. These capabilities and data might need to be shared by a variety of other services.

A prime example of this principle is a user identity service, which simply provides information about specific users of the system. This is illustrated in Figure 12-3.

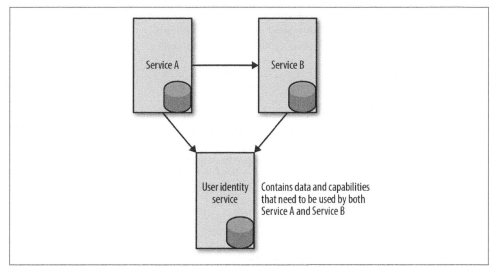

Figure 12-3. Using services to share common data with other services

There might be no complex business logic involved with this data service, but it is ultimately responsible for all the general information associated with individual users. This information often is used by a large number of other services.

Having a centralized service that provides and manages this single piece of information is highly useful.

Mixed Reasons

The preceding guidelines outline some basic criteria for determining where service boundaries should be. Often, though, it is a combination of reasons that can ultimately make the decision for you.

For example, having a single user identity service makes sense from a data ownership and shared capabilities perspective, but it might not make sense from a team ownership standpoint. Data for which it might make sense to store in a database associated with user identity might be better stored in a separate service or services.

As a specific example of such data, a user may have search preferences that are typically part of a user profile, but are not typically used by anything outside of the search infrastructure. As such, it might make sense to store this data in a search identity service that is distinct from a user identity service. This might be for data complexity reasons or even performance reasons.[1]

---

1 Why require every access to user identity information to contain search preferences if search preferences are used only in a few very specific cases?

Ultimately, you must use your judgment while also taking the preceding criteria into account. And, of course, you must also consider the business logic and requirements dictated by your company and your specific business needs.

Going Too Far

Often, though, you can go too far in splitting your application into services. Creating service boundaries using the previously discussed criteria can be taken to the extreme, and too many services can be created.

For example, rather than providing a simple user identity service, you might decide to take that simple service and further divide it into several smaller services, such as the following:

- User human readable name service
- User physical address management service
- User email address management service
- User hometown management service
- User … management service

Doing this is most likely splitting things up too far.[2]

There are several problems with splitting services into too fine a number of pieces, including overall application performance. But at the most fundamental, every time you split a piece of functionality into multiple services, you do the following:

- Decrease the complexity of the individual services (usually).
- Increase the complexity of your application as a whole.

The smaller service size typically makes individual services less complicated. However, the more services you have, the larger the number of independent services that need to be coordinated and the more complex your overall application architecture becomes.

Having a system with an excessively large number of services tends to create the following problems in your application:

Big picture
    It becomes more difficult to keep the entire application architecture in mind, because the application is becoming more complicated.

---

2 OK, forget "most likely" goes too far. This example "most certainly" goes too far in splitting things up.

More failure opportunities
> More independent components need to work together, creating more opportunity for interservice failures to occur.

Harder to change services
> Each individual service tends to have more consumers of that service. Having more service consumers increases the likelihood of changes to your service negatively affecting one of your consumers.

More dependencies
> Each individual service tends to have more dependencies on other services. More dependencies means more places for problems to occur.

Many of these problems can be mitigated by defining solid interface boundaries between services, but this is not a complete solution.

The Right Balance

Ultimately, deciding on the proper number of services and the proper size of each service is a complicated problem to solve. It requires careful consideration of the balance between the advantages of creating more services and the disadvantages of creating a more complex system as a whole.

Building too few services will create problems similar to the monolith application, where too many developers will be working on a single service and the individual services themselves become overly complicated.

Building too many services will cause individual services to become trivially simple, but the overall application becomes overly complicated with complex interactions between the services. I've actually heard of an example application utilizing microservices that defined a "Yes" service and a "No" service that simply returned those boolean results—this is extreme taken to extreme. It would be great to define exactly what the *right* size is for a service, but it depends on your application and your company culture. The best advice is to keep this complexity trade-off in mind as you define your services and your architecture.

Finding the appropriate balance for your specific application, organization, and company culture is important in making the most use of a service-based environment.

CHAPTER 13

Dealing with Service Failures

One of the vulnerabilities in building a large microservice-based application is dealing with service failures. The more services you have, the greater the likelihood of a service failing, and the larger number of other services that are dependent on the failed service.

Cascading Service Failures

Consider a service that you own. It has several dependencies, and several services depend on it. Figure 13-1 illustrates the service "Our Service" with multiple dependencies (Service A, Service B, and Service C) and several services that depend on it (Consumer 1 and Consumer 2).

What happens if one of our dependencies fails? Figure 13-2 shows Service A failing.

Unless you are careful, this can cause "Our Service" to fail, and that failure can cause Consumer 1 and Consumer 2 to fail. The error can cascade, as shown in Figure 13-3.

A single service in your system can, if unchecked, cause serious problems to your entire application.

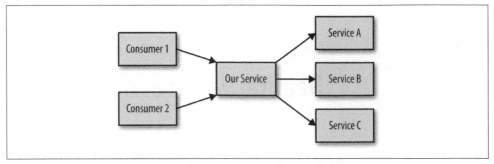

Figure 13-1. Our Service and its dependencies and consumers

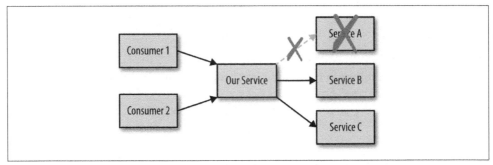

Figure 13-2. Our Service with a failed dependency

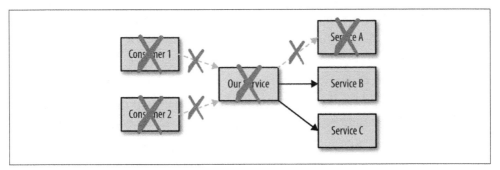

Figure 13-3. Cascading failure

What can you do to prevent cascading failures from occurring? There are times when you can do nothing—a service error in a dependency will cause you (and other dependent services) to fail, because of the high level of dependency required. Sometimes your service can't do its job if a dependency has failed. But that isn't always the case. In fact, often there is plenty you can do to salvage your service's actions for the case in which a dependent service fails. In this chapter, we will discuss some of these techniques.

Responding to a Service Failure

When a service you depend on fails, how should you respond? As a service developer, your response to a dependency failure must be:

- Predictable
- Understandable
- Reasonable for the situation

Let's look at each of these.

Predictable Response

Having a predictable response is an important aspect for services to be able to depend on other services. You must provide a predictable response given a specific set of circumstances and requests. This is critical to avoid the previously described cascading service failures from affecting every aspect of your application. Even a small failure in such an environment can cascade and grow into a large problem if you are not careful.

As such, if one of your downstream dependencies fails, you still have a responsibility to generate a predictable response. Now that predictable response might be an error message. That is an acceptable response, as long as there is an appropriate error mechanism included in your API to allow generating such an error response.

An error response is *not* the same as an unpredictable response. An unpredictable response is a response that is not expected by the services you are serving. An error response is a valid response stating that you were not able to perform the specified request. They are two different things.

If your service is asked to perform the operation "3 + 5," it is expected to return a number, specifically the number "8." This is a predictable response. If your service is asked to perform the operation "5 / 0," a predictable response would be "Not a Number," or "Error, invalid request." That is a predictable response. An unpredictable response would be if you returned "50000000000" once and "38393384384337" another time (sometimes described as *garbage in, garbage out*).

A garbage in, garbage out response is not a predictable response. A predictable response to garbage in would be "invalid request."

Your upstream dependencies expect you to provide a predictable response. Don't output garbage if you've been given garbage as input. If you provide an unpredictable response to an unpredictable reaction from a downstream service, you just propagate the unpredictable nature up the value chain. Sooner or later, that unpredictable reaction will be visible to your customers, which will affect your business. Or, worse, the unpredictable response injects invalid data into your business processes, which makes your business processes inconsistent and invalid. This can affect your business analytics as well as promote a negative customer experience.

As much as possible, even if your dependencies fail or act unpredictably, it is important that you do not propagate that unpredictability upward to those who depend on you.

 A predictable response really means a planned response. Don't think "Well, if a dependency fails, I can't do anything so I might just as well fail, too." If everything else is failing, you should instead, *proactively* figure out what a reasonable response would be to the situation. Then detect the situation and perform the expected response.

Understandable Response

Understandable means that you have an agreed upon format and structure for your responses with your upstream processes. This constitutes a contract between you and your upstream services. Your response must fit within the bounds of that contract, even if you have misbehaving dependencies. It is never acceptable for you to violate your API contract with your consumers just because a dependency violated its API contract with you. Instead, make sure your contracted interface provides enough support to cover all contingencies of action on your part, including that of failed dependencies.

Reasonable Response

Your response should be indicative of what is actually happening with your service. When asked "What is 3 + 5?" it should not return "red" even if dependencies are failing. It *might* be acceptable to return "Sorry, I couldn't calculate that result," or "Please try again later," but it should not return "red" as the answer.

Problems with Unreasonable API Responses

This sounds obvious, but you'd be surprised by the number of times an unreasonable response can cause problems. Imagine, for instance, if a service wants to get a list of all accounts that are expired and ready to be deleted. As illustrated in Figure 13-4, you might call an "expired account" service (which will return a list of accounts to be deleted), and then go out and delete all the accounts in the list.

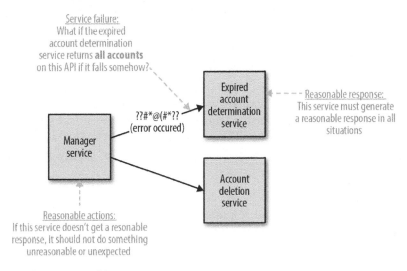

Figure 13-4. Unreasonable API response

If the "expired account" service runs into a problem and cannot calculate a valid response, it should return "None," or "I'm sorry, I can't do that right now." Imagine the problems it would cause if, instead of returning a reasonable response, it returned a list of *all* accounts in the system—well, you can see where this ends up.[1]

Determining Failures

How do you determine when a dependency is failing? It depends on the failure mode. Here are some example failure modes that are important to consider:

Garbled response
> The response was not understandable. It was "garbage" data in an unrecognizable format. This might indicate that the response is in the wrong format or the format might have syntax errors in it.

---

1 Yes, this sort of problem really occurs to real systems. And, yes, it is scary.

Response indicated a fatal error occurred
> The response was understandable. It indicated that a serious error occurred processing the request. This is usually not a failure of the network communications layer, but of the service itself. It could also be caused by the request sent to the service not being understandable.

Result was understandable but didn't match needed result
> The response was understandable. It indicated that the operation was performed successfully without serious errors, but the data returned did not match what was expected to be returned.

Result out of expected bounds
> The response was understandable. It indicated that the operation was performed successfully without serious errors. The data returned was of a reasonable and expected format, but the data itself was not within expected bounds. For example, consider a service call that is requesting the number of days since the first of the year. What happens if it returns a number such as 843? That would be a result that is understandable, parsable, did not fail, but is clearly not within the expected bounds.

Response did not arrive
> The request was sent, but no response ever arrived from the service. This could happen as a result of a network communications problem, a service problem, or a service outage.

Response was slow in arriving
> The request was sent, and the response was received. The response was valuable and useful, and within expected bounds. However, the response came much later than expected. This is often an indication that the service or network is overloaded, or that other resource allocation issue exists.

These are generally ordered from the easiest to detect to the most difficult. When you receive a response that is garbled, you instantly know the response is not usable and can take appropriate action. An understandable response that did not match the needed results can be a bit more challenging to detect, and the appropriate action to take can be tougher to determine, but it is still reasonable to do so.

A response that never arrives is difficult to detect in a way that allows you to perform an appropriate action with the result. If all you are going to do is generate an error response to your consumer, a simple timeout on your dependency may suffice in catching the missing response.

A Better Approach to Catch Responses That Never Arrive

This doesn't always work, however. For instance, what do you do if a service usually takes 50 ms to respond, but the variation can cause the response to come as quick as 10 ms, or take as long as 500 ms? What do you set your timeout to? An obvious answer is something greater than 500 ms. But, what if your contracted response time to the consumer of your service is <150 ms? Obviously, a simple timeout of 500 ms isn't reasonable, as that is effectively the same as you simply passing your dependency error on to your consumer. This violates the *predictable* and the *understandable* tests.

How can you resolve this issue? One potential answer is to use a *circuit breaker* pattern. This coding pattern involves your service keeping track of calls to your dependency and how many of them succeed versus how many fail (or timeout). If a certain threshold of failures is reached, the circuit breaker "breaks" and causes your service to assume your dependency is down and stop sending requests or expecting responses from the service. This allows your service to immediately detect the failure and take appropriate action, which can save your upstream latency SLAs.

You can then periodically check your dependency by sending a request to it that is known to fail. If it begins to succeed again (above a predefined threshold), the circuit breaker is "reset" and your service can resume using the dependency again.

A response that comes in slow from a service (versus never comes in) is perhaps the most difficult to detect. The problem becomes how slow is too slow? This can be a tough question and simply using basic timeouts (with or without circuit breakers) is usually insufficient to reasonably handle this situation, because a slow response can "sometimes" be fast enough, generating seemingly erratic results. Remember, *predictability* of response is an important characteristic for your service, and a dependency that fails unpredictably (because of slow responses and bad timeouts) will hurt your ability to create a predictable response to your dependencies.

Greater Sophistication in Detecting Slow Dependencies

A more sophisticated timeout mechanism, along with circuit breaker and similar patterns, can help with this situation. For instance, perhaps you can create "buckets" for catching the recent performance of calls to a given dependency. Each time you call the dependency, you store this fact into a bucket based on how long the response took to arrive. You keep results in the buckets for a specific period of time only. Then, you use these bucket counts to create rules for triggering the circuit breaker. For instance, you could create these rules:

- If you receive "500 requests in one minute that take longer than 150 ms," you trigger the circuit breaker.
- If you receive "50 requests in one minute that take longer than 500 ms," trigger the circuit breaker.
- If "you receive 5 requests in one minute that take longer than 1,000 ms," trigger the circuit breaker.

This type of layered technique can catch more serious slowdowns earlier while not ignoring less serious slowdowns.

Appropriate Action

What do you do if an error occurs? That depends on the error. The following are some useful patterns that you can employ for handling errors of various types.

Graceful Degradation

If a service dependency fails, can your service live without the response? Can it continue performing the work it needs to do, just without the response from the failed service? If your service can perform at least a limited portion of what it was expected to do without the response from the failed service, this is an example of *graceful degradation*.

Graceful degradation is when a service reduces the amount of work it can accomplish as little as possible when it lacks needed results from a failed service.

Example 13-1. Reduced functionality

Imagine that you have a web application that generates an ecommerce website that sells T-shirts. Let's also assume that there is an "image service" that provides URLs for images to be displayed on this website. If the application makes a call to this image service and the service fails, what should the application do? One option would be for the application to continue displaying the requested product to the customer, but without the images of the product (or show a "no image available" message). The web application can continue to operate as an ecommerce store, just with the reduced capability of not being able to display product images.

This is far superior to the ecommerce website simply failing and returning an error to the user simply because the images are not available.

This is an example of *reduced functionality*.

It is important for a service (or application) to provide as much value as it can, even if not all the data it normally would need is available to it due to a dependency failure.

Graceful Backoff

There comes a point at which there just aren't enough results available to be useful. The request must simply fail. Instead of generating an error message, can you perform some other action that will provide value to the consumer of your service?

Example 13-2. Graceful backoff

Continuing with the situation described in Example 13-1, suppose that the service that provides all the details for a given product has failed. This means that the website doesn't have any information it can display about the requested product. It doesn't make any sense to simply show an empty page, as that is not useful to your customers. It is also not a good idea to generate an error ("I'm sorry, an error occurred").

Instead, you could display a page that apologizes for the problem, but provides links to the most popular products available on the site. Although this is not what the customer really wanted, it is potentially of value to the customer, and it prevents a simple "page failed" error from occurring.

Changing what you need to do in a way that provides some value to the consumer, even if you cannot really complete the request, is an example of *graceful backoff*.

Fail as Early as Possible

What if it is not possible for your service to continue to operate without the response from the failed service? What if there are no reduced functionality or graceful backoff options that make sense? Without the response from the failed service, you can't do anything reasonable. In this case, you might just need to fail the request.

If you have determined that there is nothing you can do to save a request from failing, it is important that you fail the request as soon as possible. Do not go about doing other actions or tasks that are part of the original request after you know the request will fail.

A corollary to this rule is to perform as many checks on an inbound request as possible and as early as possible in order to ensure that, when you move forward, there is a good chance that the request will succeed.

 Consider the service that takes two integers and divides them. You know that it is invalid to divide a number by zero. If you get a request such as "3 / 0," you could try to calculate the result. Sooner or later in the calculation process, you'll notice that the result can't be generated, and you will issue an error.

Because you know that all divisions by zero will always fail, simply check the data that is passed into the request. If the divisor is zero, return an error immediately. There is no reason to attempt the calculation.

Why should you fail as early as possible? There are a few reasons:

Resource conservation
If a request will fail, all work you do before you determine that the request will fail is wasted work. If that work involves making many calls to dependent services, you could waste significant resources only to get an error.

Responsiveness
The sooner you determine a request will fail, the sooner you can give that result to the requester. This lets the requester move on and make other decisions more quickly.

Error complexity
Sometimes, if you let a failing request move forward, the way it fails might be a more complex situation that is more difficult to diagnose or more evasive. For instance, consider the "3 / 0" example. You can determine immediately that the calculation will fail and can return that. If you instead go ahead and perform the calculation, the error will occur, but perhaps in a more complicated manner—for example, depending on the algorithm you use to do the division, you could get caught in an infinite loop that only ends when a timeout occurs.[2]

Thus, instead of getting an error such as "divide by zero" error, you would wait a very long time and get an "operation timeout" error. Which error would be more useful in diagnosing the problem?

---

2 A classic example of a division operation that could act this way is by using the successive subtraction approach to division. Unless caught ahead of time, a division by zero using this algorithm can create an infinite loop.

Customer-Caused Problems

It is especially important to fail as early as possible for cases that involve invalid input coming from the consumer of your service. If you know that there are limits to what your service can do reasonably, check for those limits as early as possible.

A real-world resource wasting example of "fail as early as possible"

At a company I once worked with, there was an account service that was having performance problems. The service began slowing down and slowing down until it was mostly unusable.

After digging into the problem, we discovered that someone had sent the account service a bad request. Someone had asked the account service to get a list of 100,000 customer accounts, with all the account details.

Now, there is no legitimate business use case for this to have happened (in this context), so the request itself was obviously an invalid request. The value 100,000 was way out of range of rational numbers to provide as input to this request.

However, the account service dutifully attempted to process the request…and processed…and processed…and processed…

The service eventually failed because it did not have enough resources to complete such a large request. It stopped after processing a few thousand accounts and returned a simple error message.

The calling service, the one that generated the invalid request, saw the failure message and decided that it should just retry the request. And retry. And retry. And retry.

The account service repeatedly processed thousands of accounts only to have those results thrown away in a failure message. But it did this over and over and over again.

The repeated failed requests consumed large quantities of available resources. It consumed so many resources that legitimate requests to the service began to back up, and eventually fail.

A simple check early on in the account service's processing of the request (such as a check to ensure that the requested number of accounts was of a reasonable size) could have avoided the excessive and ultimately wasted consumption of resources. Additionally, if the error message returned indicated that the error was permanent and caused by an invalid argument, the calling service could have seen the "permanent error" indicator and not attempted retries that it knew would fail.

Provide service limits

A corollary to this story is to always provide service limits. If you know your service can't handle retrieving more than, say, 5,000 accounts at a time, state that limit in your service contract and test and fail any request that is outside that limit.

PART IV

Scaling Applications

Even sea snails can scale.

CHAPTER 14

Two Mistakes High

Surely, this is OK…

Consider the following anecdote I once overheard:

> We were wondering how changing a setting on our MySQL database might impact our performance, but we were worried that the change might cause our production database to fail. Because we didn't want to bring down production, we decided to make the change to our backup (replica) database, instead. After all, it wasn't being used for anything at the moment.

Makes sense, right? Have you ever heard this rationale before?

Well, the problem here is that the database *was* being used for something. It was being used to provide a backup for production. Except, it couldn't be used that way anymore.

You see, the backup database was essentially being used as an experimental playground for trying different types of settings. The net result was that the backup database began to *drift* away from the primary production database as settings began to change over time.

Then, one day, the inevitable happened.

The production database failed.

The backup database initially did what it was supposed to do. It took over the job of the primary database. Except, it really couldn't. The settings on the backup database had wandered so far away from those required by the primary database that it could no longer reliably handle the same traffic load that the primary database handled.

The backup database slowly failed, and the site went down.

This is a true story. It's a story about best intentions. You have a backup, replicated database on standby. It's ready to take over as needed when the primary database fails. Except, that the backup database wasn't treated with the same respect as the primary database, and it loses the ability to perform its main purposes, that of being the backup database.

Two wrongs don't make a right, two mistakes don't negate each other, and two problems don't self-correct. A primary database failure along with a poorly managed backup server does not create a good day.

What Is "Two Mistakes High"?

If you've ever flown radio control (R/C) airplanes before, you might have heard the expression "keep your plane two mistakes high."

When you learn to fly R/C planes, especially when you began learning how to do acrobatics, you learn this quickly. You see, mistakes equate to altitude. You make a mistake, you lose altitude. You lose too much altitude, and well, badness happens. Keeping your plane "two mistakes high" means keeping it high enough that you have enough altitude to recover from two, independent mistakes.

Why two mistakes? Simple. You always want to be operating your plane high enough so that you can recover if (when) you make a mistake. Now, suppose that you make a mistake and lose a bunch of altitude. During your recovery from that mistake, you also want to be high enough that you can recover from a mistake. Think about it: during your recovery process, you are typically stressed and perhaps in an awkward situation doing potentially abnormal things—just the type of situation that can cause you to make another mistake. If you aren't high enough, you can crash.

Put another way, if you normally fly two mistakes high, you can always have a backup plan for recovering from a mistake, even if you are currently recovering from a mistake.

This same philosophy is important to understand when building highly available, high-scale applications.

How do we "keep two mistakes high" in an application? For starters, when we identify the failure scenarios that we anticipate our application facing, we walk through the ramifications of those scenarios and our recovery plan for them. We make sure the recovery plan itself does not have mistakes or other shortcomings built into it—in short, we check that the recovery plan is able to work. If we find that it doesn't work, then it's not a recovery plan.

"Two Mistakes High" in Practice

This is just one potential scenario for which "two mistakes" applies. There are many more. Let's take a look at some example scenarios to see how this philosophy plays out in our applications.

Losing a Node

Let's look at an example scenario involving traffic to a web service.

Example 14-1. How many nodes are needed?

Suppose that you're building a service that is designed to handle 1,000 requests per second (req/sec). Further, let's assume that a single node in your service can handle 300 req/sec.

Question: How many nodes do you need to handle your traffic demands?

Some basic math should come up with a good answer:

$$number\_of\_nodes\_needed = \left\lceil \frac{number\_of\_requests}{requests\_per\_node} \right\rceil$$

where:

number_of nodes_needed
  The number of nodes needed to handle the specified number of requests.

number_of_requests
  The design limit for the amount of requests the service is expected to happen.

requests_per_node
  The expected average number of requests each node in the service can handle.

Putting in our numbers:

$$number\_of\_nodes\_needed = \left\lceil \frac{1000\ req/sec}{300\ req/sec} \right\rceil = \lceil 3.3 \rceil = 4\ nodes$$

$$number\_of\_nodes\_needed = 4\ nodes$$

You need four nodes in your service to handle the 1,000 req/sec expected service load. Switching this around, using four nodes, each node will handle:

$$requests\_per\_node = \frac{number\_of\_requests}{number\_of\_nodes}$$

$$requests\_per\_node = \frac{1,000 \ req/sec}{4 \ nodes} = 250 \ req/sec/node$$

Each node will handle 250 req/sec, which is well below your 300 req/sec per node limit.

You have four nodes in your system. You can handle the expected traffic, and because you have four nodes, you can handle the loss of a node. You have built in the ability to handle a node failure. Right? *Right???*

Well, no, not really. If you lose a node at peak traffic, your service will begin to fail. Why? Because if you lose a node, the rest of your traffic must be spread among the remaining three nodes, and as illustrated in Example 14-2, that just won't work:

Example 14-2. Losing a node

In the system in Example 14-1, if you lose one of the four nodes, you have only three remaining to handle the traffic. So:

$$requests\_per\_node = \frac{number\_of\_requests}{number\_of\_nodes}$$

$$requests\_per\_node = \frac{1000 \ req/sec}{3 \ nodes} = 333 \ req/sec/node$$

That's 333 req/sec per node, which is well above your 300 req/sec node limit.

Because each node can handle only 300 req/sec, you have overloaded your servers. Either you will give poor performance to all your customers, or you will drop some requests, or you will begin to fail in other ways. In any case, you will begin to lose availability.

As you can see, if you lose a node in your system, you cannot continue to operate at full capacity. So, even though you think you can recover from a node failure, you really can't. You are vulnerable.

To handle a node failure, you need more than four nodes. If you want to be able to handle a single node failure, you need five nodes. That way, if one of the five nodes fail, you still have four remaining nodes to handle the load, as shown in Example 14-3.

Example 14-3. Losing a node with spare capacity

If you lose one of your *five* available nodes, leaving *four* nodes, you then have:

$$requests\_per\_node = \frac{number\_of\_requests}{number\_of\_nodes}$$

$$requests\_per\_node = \frac{1000 \ req/sec}{4 \ nodes} = 250 \ req/sec/node$$

Because this value is below the node limit of 300 req/sec, there is enough capacity to continue handling all of your traffic, even with a single node failure.

Problems During Upgrades

Upgrades and routine maintenance can cause availability problems beyond just the obvious. Take a look at Example 14-4.

Example 14-4. Upgrading your application

Suppose that you have a service whose average traffic is 1,000 req/sec. Further, let's assume that a single node in your service can handle 300 req/sec. As discussed in Example 14-1, four nodes is the required minimum to run your service. To handle the expected traffic and to be able to handle a single node failure, you give your service five nodes with which to handle the load.

Now, suppose that you want to do a software upgrade to the service running on the nodes. To keep your service operating at full capacity during the upgrade, you decide to do a *rolling deploy*.

Put simply, a rolling deploy means that you upgrade one node at a time (temporarily taking it offline to perform the upgrade). After the first node has been upgraded successfully and is handling traffic again, you move on to upgrade the second node (temporarily taking it offline). You continue until all five nodes are upgraded.

Because only one node is offline to be upgraded at any point in time, there are always at least four nodes handling traffic. Because four nodes is enough to handle all of your traffic, your service stays up and operational during the upgrade.

This is a great plan. You've built a system that not only can handle a single node failure, but it also can be upgraded by rolling deploys without having any downtime.

But what happens if a single node failure occurs *during* an upgrade? In that case, you have one node unavailable for the upgrade, and one node failed. That leaves only three nodes to handle all your traffic, which is not enough. You are experiencing a service degradation or outage.

But, what's the likelihood of a node failure occurring during an upgrade?

How many times have you had an upgrade fail? In fact, an argument can be made that you are *more* prone to node failures around the time of an upgrade than at any other point in time. The upgrade and the node failure do not have to be independent.

 The lesson is this: even if you think you have redundancy to handle different failure modes, if it is likely that two or more problems can occur at the same time (because the problems are correlated), you essentially do not have redundancy at all. You are prone to an availability issue.

So, in summary, for the system in Example 14-1, to handle the 1,000 req/sec expected traffic using nodes that can handle 300 req/sec each, we need:

Four nodes
Which can handle the traffic but will not handle a node failure.

Five nodes
Which handles a single node failure, or makes it possible for a node to be unavailable for maintenance or upgrade.

Six nodes
Which can handle a multinode failure, or makes it possible for you to survive single node failures while another node is down for maintenance or upgrade.

Data Center Resiliency

Let's scale the problem up a bit and take a look at data center redundancy and resilience.

Example 14-5. A larger service

Suppose that your service is now handling 10,000 req/sec. With single nodes handling 300 req/sec, that means you need 34 nodes, without considering redundancy for failures and upgrades.

Let's add a bunch of resiliency and use a total of 40 nodes (each handling 250 req/sec), which allows for plenty of extra capacity. We could lose up to six nodes, and still handle our full capacity.

Let's do an even better job: let's split those 40 nodes evenly across four data centers so that we have even more redundancy.

So, now we are resilient to data center outages as well as node failures.

Right?

Well, good question. Obviously, we can handle individual node outages, because we have given ourselves 6 (40 – 34) extra nodes. But what if a data center goes offline?

If a single data center fails, we lose one quarter of our servers. In this example, we would go from 40 nodes to 30 nodes. Each node no longer must handle traffic of 250 req/sec; rather, they need to handle 334 req/sec. Because this is more than the capacity of your fictitious nodes, you have an availability issue.

Although we used multiple data centers, a failure of just one of those data centers would leave us in a situation where we wouldn't be able to handle increased traffic. We think we are resilient to a data center loss, but we are not.

Then, how many servers *do* you need?

How many servers do we need to have the ability to lose a data center? Let's find out.

Using the same assumptions as Example 14-5, we know that we need a minimum of 34 working servers to handle all of our traffic. If we are using four data centers, how many servers do we need to have true data center redundancy?

Well, we need to make sure we always have 34 working servers, even if one of the four data centers goes down. This means that we need to have 34 servers spread across three data centers:

$$nodes\_per\_data\_center - \left\lceil \frac{minimum\_number\_of\_servers}{number\_of\_data\_centers - 1} \right\rceil$$

$$nodes\_per\_data\_center = \left\lceil \frac{34}{4 - 1} \right\rceil$$

$$nodes\_per\_data\_center = \lceil 11.333 \rceil = 12 \; servers/data\_center$$

Because we need 12 servers per data center, and because any one of the four data centers could go offline, we need 12 in *each* data center:

$$total\_nodes = nodes\_per\_data\_center * 4 = 48 \; nodes$$

We need 48 nodes to guarantee that you have 34 working servers in the case of a data center outage.

How does changing the number of data centers change our calculation? Let's take a look at Example 14-6.

Example 14-6. Different number of data centers

What if we have two data centers? As before:

$$nodes\_per\_data\_center = \left\lceil \frac{minimum\_number\_of\_servers}{number\_of\_data\_centers - 1} \right\rceil$$

$$nodes\_per\_data\_center = \left\lceil \frac{34}{2 - 1} \right\rceil$$

$$nodes\_per\_data\_center = 34$$

$$total\_nodes = nodes\_per\_data\_center * 2 = 68 \ nodes$$

If we have two data centers, we need 68 nodes. How about some other situations. If you have:

Four data centers
> We need 48 nodes to maintain data center redundancy.

Six data centers
> We need 42 nodes to maintain data center redundancy.

This demonstrates the seemingly odd conclusion: to provide the ability to recover from an entire data center outage, the more data centers you have, the fewer nodes you need overall spread across those data centers. So much for natural intuition.

 The lesson is this: although the details of this demonstration might not directly apply to real-world situations, the point still applies. Be careful when you devise your resiliency plans. Your intuition might not match reality, and if your intuition is wrong, you are prone to an availability issue.

Hidden Shared Failure Types

Sometimes, multiple problem scenarios that seem to be independent and not likely to occur together are, in fact, dependent scenarios. This means that they could, and in some situations, reasonably should be expected to fail together.

Example 14-7. Racking

Suppose that your service runs on four nodes. You are trying to think ahead, so you use a total of six nodes—enough to handle both a single node failure and an upgrade in progress.

You're all set. Your system is safe.

Then, it happens: in your data center, a power supply in a rack goes bad, and the rack goes dark.

It's usually about this time that you realize that all six of your servers are in the same rack. How do you discover this? Because all six servers go down, and your service is completely down.

There goes redundancy…

Even when you think you are safe, you might not be. We know that not all problems are independent of one another. But this is a case where a potentially unseen, or at least unnoticed, commonality exists between all your servers: they all share the same rack and the same power supply for that rack.

 The lesson is this: check for the hidden shared failure modes that can cause your carefully laid plans to be wrong, thus making you prone to an availability issue.

Failure Loops

Failure loops are when a specific problem causes your system to fail in a way that makes it difficult or impossible for you to fix the problem without causing a worse problem to occur.

The best way to explain this is with a non-server-based example:

Example 14-8. A garage door

Suppose you live in a great apartment that even provides an enclosed garage for you to store things! Wow, you are set.

But the power in the place goes out a lot, so you decide to buy a generator that you can use when the power does go out. You take the generator, and the gas it uses, and you store it in the garage. Life is good.

Then, when the power goes out, you go to get your generator.

That's when you realize for the first time that the only way to access your garage is through the electric-powered garage door—the one that doesn't work because the power is out.

Oops.

Just because you have a backup plan does not mean you can implement the backup plan when needed.

The same issues can apply to our service world. Can a service failure make it difficult to repair that same service because it caused some other seemingly unrelated issue to occur?

For example, if your service fails, how easy is it to deploy an updated version of your service? What happens if your service-deployment service fails? What about if the service you use to monitor the performance of other services fails?

 The lesson is this: make sure the plans you have for recovering from a problem can be implemented even when the problem is occurring. Dependent relationships between the problem and the solution to the problem can make you prone to an availability issue.

Managing Your Applications

"Fly two mistakes high" in our context means *don't just look for the surface failure modes.* Look the next level down. Make sure that you do not have dependent failure modes and that the recovery mechanisms you have put in place will, in fact, recover your system while a failure is going on.

Additionally, don't ignore problems. They don't go away and they can interfere with your predicted availability plans. Just because the database that fails is only the backup database, doesn't mean it isn't mission-critical to fix. Treat your backup and redundant systems just as preciously as you treat your primary systems. After all, they are just as important.

As a friend of mine is often heard saying, "if it touches production, it is production." Don't take anything in production for granted.

This stuff is difficult. It isn't at all obvious to know when you have these types of layered or dependent failures. Take the time to look at your situations and resolve them.

The Space Shuttle

Let's end this chapter with a great example of an independent, redundant, multilevel error-recoverable system. In fact, it was one of the very first large-scale software applications that utilized extreme principles of redundancy and failure management. It had to—the astronauts' lives depended on it.

I'm referring to the United States Space Shuttle program.

The Space Shuttle program had some significant and serious mechanical problems, which we won't fully address here. But the software system built into the Space Shuttle utilized state-of-the art techniques for redundancy and independent error recovery.

The primary computer system of the Space Shuttle consisted of five computers. Four of them were identical computers with identical software running on them, but the fifth was different. We'll discuss that later.

The four main computers all ran the exact same program during critical parts of the mission (such as launch and landing). The four computers were all given the same data and had the same software, and were expected to generate the same results. All four performed the same calculations, and they constantly compared the results. If, at any point in time, any of the computers generated a different result, the four computers voted on which result was correct. The winning result was used, and the computer(s) that generated the losing result were turned off for the duration of the flight. The shuttle could successfully fly with only three computers turned on, and it could safely land with only two operational computers.

Talk about the ultimate in democratic systems. The winners rule, and the losers are terminated.

But what would happen if the four computers couldn't agree? This could happen if there was multiple failures and multiple computers had been shut down. Or, it could happen if a serious software glitch in the main software affected all four computers at the same time (the four computers were running the exact same software, after all).

This is where the fifth computer came into play. It normally sat idle, but if needed, it could perform the exact same calculations as the other four. The key was the software it ran. The software for the fifth system was a much simpler version of the software that was built by a completely independent group of programmers. In theory, it could not have the same software errors as the main software.

So, if the main software and the four main computers could not agree on a result, it left the final result to the fifth, completely independent computer.

This is a highly redundant, high availability system with a high level of separation between potential problems.

During its 30 years of operation, the Space Shuttle program never experienced a serious life-threatening problem during any of its missions that was a result of the failure of the software or the computers they ran—even though the software was, at the time, the most complex software system ever built for a space program to use.

CHAPTER 15

Service Ownership

Chapter 12 stated that a service must be owned and maintained by a single development team within your organization, but we didn't delve deeply into the specifics of what this means. In this chapter, we will explain what is meant by *service ownership*, and what is necessary for a *Single Team Owned Service Architecture* to work.

Single Team Owned Service Architecture

What is Single Team Owned Service Architecture (STOSA)? STOSA is an important guiding principle for large organizations that have many development teams that own and manage services comprising one or more applications.

What does it mean to have a STOSA application and organization? To be STOSA, you must meet the following criteria:

- Have an application that is constructed using a service-based architecture or a microservice-based architecture.
- Have multiple development teams that are responsible for building and maintaining the application.
- All services in your application must be assigned to a development team.
- No service should be assigned to more than one development team.
- Individual development teams may own more than one service.
- Teams are responsible for all aspects of managing the service, from service architecture and design, through development, testing, deployment, monitoring, and incident resolution.
- Services have strong boundaries between them, including well-documented APIs.

- Services maintain internal service-level agreements (SLAs) between them that are monitored and violations reported to the owning team.

A *STOSA-based application* is an application for which all services follow the preceding rules. A *STOSA-based organization* is one in which all service teams follow the preceding rules and all applications are STOSA applications.

Typically, in a STOSA-based organization, each team should be of reasonable size (typically between three and eight engineers). If a team is too small, it cannot manage a service effectively. If it's too large, it becomes cumbersome to manage the team.

Figure 15-1 shows a typical STOSA-based organization managing a STOSA application.

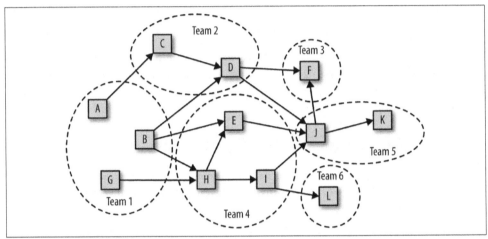

Figure 15-1. STOSA-based organization with a STOSA application

In this diagram, the boxes labeled A though L represent each individual service. The ovals represent development teams that own the enclosed services.

This application contains 12 services managed by five teams. You'll notice that each service is managed by a single team, but several teams manage more than one service. Every service has an owner, and no service has more than one owner.

Clear ownership for every aspect of the application exists. For any part of the application, you can clearly determine who is responsible and who to contact for questions, issues, or changes.

Figure 15-2 shows an example application and organization that is not a STOSA organization.

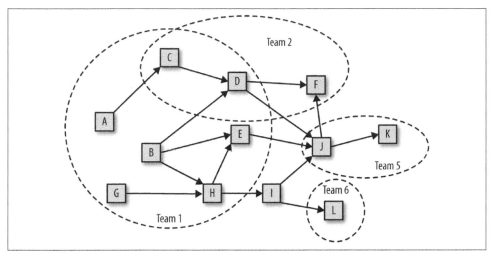

Figure 15-2. Non-STOSA-based organization

You'll notice a couple things. First, Service I does not have any owner. Yet, Services C and D are owned and maintained by more than one team.

There is no clear ownership. If you need something done in service C or D, it's not clear who is responsible. If one of those services has a problem, who responds? What happens if you need something done to service I? Who do you contact? This lack of clear ownership and responsibility makes managing a complex application even more complicated.

Advantages of a STOSA Application and Organization

As applications grow in size, they grow in complexity. A STOSA-based application can grow larger and be managed by a larger development team than a non-STOSA-based application. As such, it can scale much larger while still maintaining solid, documented, supportable interfaces.

A STOSA-based organization can handle larger and more complicated applications than a non-STOSA organization. This is because STOSA shares the complexity of a system across multiple development teams effectively, while maintaining clear ownership and lines of responsibility.

What Does it Mean to Be a Service Owner?

In a STOSA organization, the team that owns a service is ultimately 100% responsible for all aspects of that service. That team might depend on other teams for assistance (such as an operations team for hardware), but ultimately the owning team is responsible for the service.

This includes the following, specifically:

API design
> The design, implementation, testing, and version management of all APIs, internal and external, that the service exposes.

Service development
> The design, implementation, and testing of the service's business logic and business responsibilities.

Data
> The management of all data the service owns and maintains, its representation and schema, access patterns, and lifecycle.

Deployments
> The process of determining when and if a service update is required, and the deployment of new software to the service, including verification and rollback of all service nodes and the availability of the service during the deployment.

Deployment windows
> When it is safe and when it is not safe to deploy. This includes enforcing company/product-wide blackouts as well as service-specific windows.

Production changes
> All production changes needed by the service (such as load balancer settings and system tuning).

Environments
> Managing the production environment, along with all development, staging, and pre-production deployment environments for the service.

Service SLAs
> Negotiating, setting, and monitoring SLAs, along with the responsibility of keeping the service operating within those SLAs.

Monitoring
> Ensuring that monitoring is set up and managed for all appropriate aspects of the service, including monitoring service SLAs. It also is responsible for reviewing the monitoring on a regular and consistent basis.

Oncall/incident response
> Ensuring that pager events are generated when the system begins to function out of specification. Providing oncall rotation and pager management to make sure someone from the team is available to handle incidents. Handling incidents within prescribed SLA boundaries for incident responsiveness.

Reporting

Internal reporting to other teams (consumers and dependencies) as well as management reporting on the operational health of the service.

Often, the following items aren't owned by the owning team but are the responsibility of a shared infrastructure, tools, or operations team:

Servers/hardware

All hardware and infrastructure needed to run the hardware for production and all supporting environments. This is often provided by an operations team, or may be provided by a cloud provider, or both.

Tooling

Various tooling required by the owning team is often centrally owned and managed. This can include deployment tools, monitoring tools, oncall and incident response tools, and reporting tools.

Databases

The hardware and database applications used to store the data used by the service is often managed by a central team. However, the data itself, the data schema, and the use of the data, is always managed by the owning team.

Figure 15-3 shows a typical organization hierarchy for a STOSA-based organization. Essentially, all development teams that are service-owning teams are peers, organizationally. They are all supported uniformly by a series of supporting teams, including operations, tooling, databases, and other similar teams. All of these may or may not also sit on top of other core teams that have universal responsibility for the organization, but not for individual services. This can include things like an architectural guidance team or a program management team.

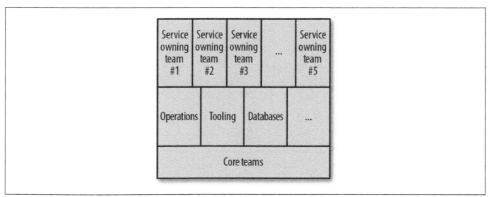

Figure 15-3. STOSA-based organization hierarchy

Service-owning teams in a STOSA organization are the teams that are ultimately responsible for all aspects of the services they own. They might depend on the core and support teams, but it is the service-owning team that is ultimately responsible for ensuring that all issues are dealt with and the service is operating properly.

For example, let's assume that a service fails because a deployment went bad due to a failure in the core deployment tool. The service failure is the responsibility of the service-owning team. They may have issues or concerns with the tooling team that they need to deal with, but ultimately the service-owning team is the one responsible for the failure. They cannot simply say "it was the tooling team's fault." Ultimately, even if that were true, it was the service that failed, and hence the service-owning team that is responsible.

With strong ownership of results also comes strong ownership of decision making affecting your service. Typically, a service-owning team is given a set of requirements they need to implement, but the details of how those requirements are implemented are their responsibility. The team might have system-wide compliance requirements they need to conform to (such as architecture guidelines or rules, tooling that must be used, or language and hardware selection restrictions), but these ultimately are part of the requirements given to them.

Beyond these requirements, all design details and decisions are the responsibility of the owning team.

Ultimately, the owning team is making a commitment to achieve an expected set of results, and maintain an appropriate set of SLAs.

CHAPTER 16

Service Tiers

Working with large, complex applications with many services can cause availability issues. A failure of a single service can cause services that depend on it to fail. This can cause a cascade effect that results in your entire application failing. This is especially egregious when the service that failed is not a mission-critical service, but it caused mission-critical services to fail.

Application Complexity

As illustrated in Figure 16-1, sometimes, the smallest and least significant of services can fail.

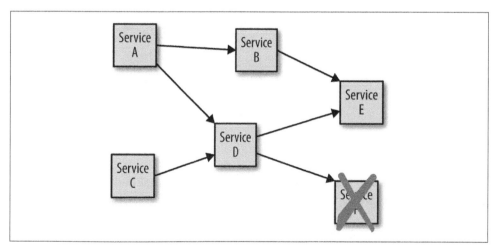

Figure 16-1. A single service failure...

This can cause your entire application to go down, as illustrated in Figure 16-2.

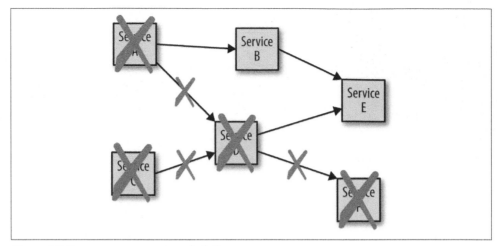

Figure 16-2. ...can cause a cascade failure

There are many ways to prevent dependent services from failing, and we discuss many of these in Chapter 13. However, adding resiliency between services also adds complexity and cost, and sometimes it is not needed. Looking at Figure 16-3, what happens if Service D is not critical to the running of Service A? Why should Service A fail simply because Service D has failed?

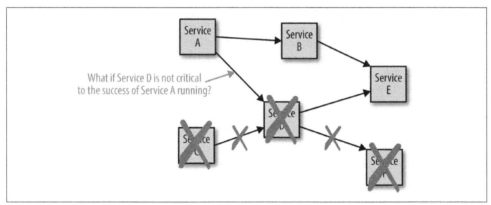

Figure 16-3. What if Service D is not critical?

How do you know when a service dependency link is critical and when it isn't? Service tiers is one way to help manage this.

What Are Service Tiers?

A service tier is simply a *label* associated with a service that indicates how critical a service is to the operation of your business. Service tiers let you distinguish between services that are mission critical, and those that are useful and helpful but not essential.

By comparing service tier levels of dependent services, you can determine which service dependencies are your most sensitive and which are less important.

Assigning Service Tier Labels to Services

All services in your system, no matter how big or how small, should be assigned a service tier. The following sections outline a scale to get you started (you can make adjustments to these recommendations as necessary to accommodate your particular business needs).

Tier 1

Tier 1 services are the most critical services in your system. A service is considered Tier 1 if a failure of that service will result in a significant impact to customers or to the company's bottom line.

The following are some examples of Tier 1 services:

Login service
  A service that lets users log in to your system.

Credit card processor
  A service that handles customer payments.

Permission service
  A service that tells you what features a given user may have access to.

Order accepting service
  A service that lets customers purchase a product on your website.

A Tier 1 service failure is a serious concern to your company.

Tier 2

A Tier 2 service is one that is important to your business but less critical than a Tier 1. A failure in a Tier 2 service can cause a degraded customer experience in a noticeable and meaningful way but does not completely prevent your customer from interacting with your system.

Tier 2 services are also services that affect your backend business processes in significant ways, but might not be directly noticeable to your customers.

The following are some examples of Tier 2 services:

Search service

A service that provides a search functionality on your website.

Order fulfillment service

A service that makes it possible for your warehouse to process an order for shipment to a customer.

A failure of a Tier 2 service will have a negative customer impact but does not represent a complete system failure.

Tier 3

A Tier 3 service is one that can have minor, unnoticeable, or difficult-to-notice customer impact, or have limited effect on your business and systems.

The following are some examples of Tier 3 services:

Customer icon service

A service that displays a customer icon or avatar on a website page.

Recommendations service

A service that displays alternate products a customer may be interested in based on what they are currently viewing.

Message of the day service

A service that displays alerts or messages to customers at the top of the web page.

Customers may or may not even notice that a Tier 3 service is failing.

Tier 4

A Tier 4 service is a service that, when it fails, causes no significant effect on the customer experience and does not significantly affect the customer's business or finances.

The following are some examples of Tier 4 services:

Sales report generator service

A service that generates a weekly sales report. Although the sales report is important, a short-term failure of the generator service will not have a significant impact.

Marketing email sending service

A service that generates emails sent regularly to your customers. If this service is down for a period of time, email generation might be delayed, but that will typically not significantly affect you or your customers.

Example: Online Store

Figure 16-4 is an example application composed of many services. It is designed for operating an online store. Each service has a label indicating the service tier assigned to each service.

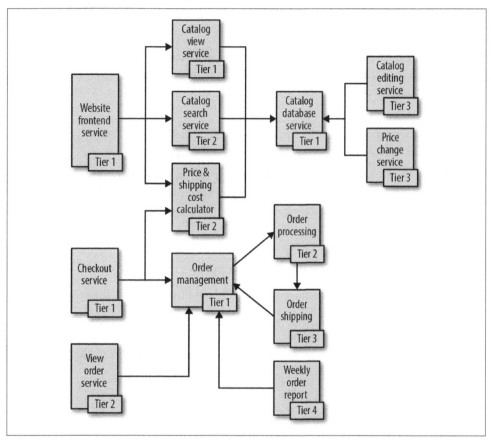

Figure 16-4. Example application: an online store

Look at this and imagine from the description what the responsibility of each service is. Imagine what the customer experience can or should be when that service is malfunctioning. The service tier should be in line with this perceived customer experience.

Here are some example services from this application for you to consider:

Website frontend service (Tier 1)
   This is the service that generates and displays the website. It generates the HTML and interacts with the user's browser for the main storefront.

This is a Tier 1 service because without it your entire online store is unavailable to your customers. It passes the Tier 1 test because if it is not available, it has a huge impact on your customers.

Catalog view service (Tier 1)

This service reads the catalog database and sends the appropriate catalog data to the frontend service. It's used to generate the detail pages that show the details of individual products in the database.

This is a Tier 1 service because without it your customers can't view any products online. It passes the Tier 1 test because if it is not available, it has a huge impact on your customers.

Catalog search service (Tier 2)

This service handles search requests from users, and returns lists of products that match the search terms.

This is a Tier 2 service because, even though search is an important customer feature to the website, it is possible for customers to browse to products and still use your site without the search bar working. The experience is obviously diminished, but it is still usable.

Catalog database service (Tier 1)

This is the database that stores the catalog itself.

This is a Tier 1 service because without the catalog database, no product can be displayed.

Catalog editing service (Tier 3)

This is the service that your employees use to add new entries to the catalog and update existing entries.

This service is considered a Tier 3 service because it is not mission critical to the ability of customers to successfully complete a purchase. Although not being able to add products to your database will affect your business, it doesn't immediately or directly affect your customers, and a bit of an outage might be acceptable.

Checkout service (Tier 1)

This is the service that displays the checkout process to your customers. Without this service, your customers can't buy products from you.

This is a Tier 1 service, because it has a significant impact on both your customers (they can't buy things) and on your business (you can't make money without customers buying things).

Order shipping service (Tier 3)

This is the service that manages the process of boxing and shipping your customers' orders (an obviously simplified example). Without this service, your customers can't receive orders they have placed.

This may seem like it should be a Tier 1 service, because shipping orders is a mission-critical aspect of your business. But think of it this way: if you can't ship orders for an hour or so, what's the impact on your customers? What about your business? In most cases, it would have very little to no impact on your customers —a one hour shipping delay wouldn't affect when customers receive their orders. It would have some effect on your business, because the employees that pack orders might not be able to do their jobs for a while. Because it has an effect on the business, but not a significant one nor a significant impact on your customers, a Tier 3 label is appropriate.

Weekly order report (Tier 4)

This is the service that gathers your ordering data and generates weekly business reports to finance and management.

This is a Tier 4 service because it has no impact on your customer's experience at all. Having a report delayed for a short period of time might affect your business, but likely not significantly.

This example should give you an idea of how you can generate appropriate service tier labels for all your services.

What's Next?

Now that you understand the various tier levels, you should be able to apply appropriate service tier labels to all of the services in your application. But now that we have our services labeled, how do we use the labels and what value do you bring? This is the topic of Chapter 17.

Using Service Tiers

After you have assigned service tiers for all your services, how do you use them? There are a few ways:

Expectations
> What is the expected uptime for the service? What is its reliability? How many problems does it have? How often is it allowed to fail?

Responsiveness
> How fast or slow should you respond to a problem, and what courses of actions are available to you in resolving the issue?

Dependencies
> What are the service tiers of your dependencies and those who depend on you, and how does that affect your service interactions?

Let's look at each of these.

Expectations

Your service's expectations are an important part of your service to your customers. Service-level agreements (SLAs) are one way to manage these expectations. This is so important that Chapter 18 is entirely dedicated to this topic.

Responsiveness

When a problem occurs in your system, your responsiveness to the issue depends on these two factors:

- The severity of the issue
- The tier of service that is having the issue

A high-severity problem on a Tier 1 service should be treated as more important than a high-severity problem on a Tier 3 service. That is clear. But if a Tier 1 service has a medium severity problem, this might need a higher level of responsiveness than a high-severity problem on a Tier 3 service. Figure 17-1 demonstrates this.

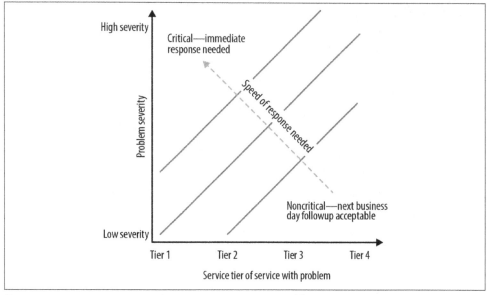

Figure 17-1. Responsiveness for service tier versus problem severity

The higher the severity of the problem, or the higher importance of the service (lower service tier number), the faster and more critical a response to the problem becomes. The parallel lines in Figure 17-1 show lines of similar response importance. A low- to medium-severity Tier 1 problem would require a similar response to an extremely high-severity Tier 3 problem. A Tier 4 problem almost never requires a critical response.

Furthermore, a low-severity Tier 2 problem would require a similar response to a high-severity Tier 4 problem.

You can use this information to adjust many aspects of your responsiveness. For example, you can use the responsiveness level to determine the following:

- Which types of problems for which services require an immediate pager notification be sent.
- The expected resolution SLAs.

- The escalation path for slow response or slow resolution.
- A schedule when a response should be provided (24 × 7 or business hours only).
- Whether emergency deployment or production changes are warranted.
- The SLAs in which your service should perform around availability and responsiveness.

Dependencies

If you are building a service, the relationship between the service tier you assign to your service and the service tier of your dependencies is significantly important. Figure 17-2 shows the relationship between your service level and that of a service dependency.

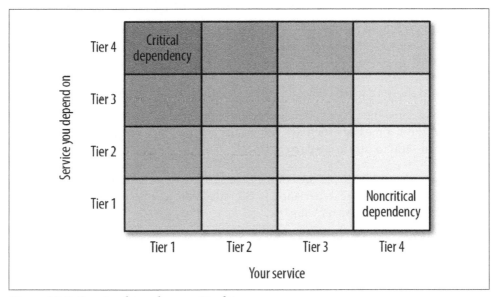

Figure 17-2. Service dependency criticality

If your service is a higher tier (lower number) than your dependent service, your dependency is a critical dependency. If your service is a lower tier (higher number) than your dependent service, your dependency is a noncritical dependency.

Critical Dependency

If, after consulting Example 17-1, you've determined that your dependency is critical, it is important that you, as a service developer, deal with failures of your dependency in a way that does not significantly affect your service.

Your service is responsible for performing as much of its capabilities as is possible if a critical dependency fails. This is because the dependency is a lower tier (higher number), which means it likely will not have the same level of availability and reliability as your service requires.

Example 17-1. Critical dependency

Looking at the application shown in Figure 16-4, focus on the website frontend service, which is a Tier 1 service. When this service tries to display a specific product detail page to a customer, it needs to determine the current price of the product. To do this, it makes calls to the price & shipping cost calculator (PSCC) service to determine the price.

What if the PSCC service (a Tier 2 service) was down? The website frontend service (a Tier 1 service) still must function as best as it can. So, what does it need to do?

It needs to gracefully handle failure messages (or lack of response) from the PSCC service. As soon as it determines that the PSCC service is down, it needs to figure out what to do in displaying the product detail page. There are a couple options:

- It could show a cached copy of the price on the page (if it had that available).
- It could show the product detail page, but not show the current price. Instead, it could show a message such as "Not available," or "Price not currently available," or even "Add to cart to see current price."

The customer can still see pictures of the product, customer reviews, and other product details. Although the experience is degraded, the customer can still complete some very important tasks on your site.

We call this *graceful degradation* (dealing with service failures was covered in greater detail in Chapter 13).

Noncritical Dependency

If, after consulting Example 17-2, you've determined that your dependency is noncritical, you can mostly ignore service failures of your dependency.

This is because your dependent service, having a higher tier (lower number), will have higher levels of availability and responsiveness than your service requires.

Example 17-2. Noncritical dependency

Again consider the online store application illustrated in Figure 16-4, but this time focus on the weekly order report service, which is a Tier 4 service. For it to get the information it needs to generate its report, it makes calls to the order management service, which is a Tier 1 service.

What happens if the order management service is down? What should the weekly order report service do? Well, it's probably reasonable for the weekly order report service to simply fail, as well. Given that the order management service is a Tier 1 service, any problems it will have will be dealt with very quickly, with a high responsiveness and high sense of urgency—much higher than would be needed to deal with the failure of the weekly order report service.

As such, the weekly order report does not need to do anything special to deal with an outage of the order management service, because it is OK for the weekly order report to simply not operate if the order management service is not available.

Summary

Service tiers provide a convenient way of expressing the criticality of a service to the service's owners, dependencies, and consumers. They provide a way of understanding expectations between services in a manner that is simple to understand and communicate. Simplicity reduces the chance of mistakes, and service tiers provide a simple model for communicating expectations in a manner designed to be easy to understand and easy to utilize.

CHAPTER 18

Service-Level Agreements

Expectation management.

That's what Service Level Agreements are all about. As discussed in Chapter 17, each service has different expectations around it. Many of these expectations are tied to the *service tier* of the service, but when we look deeper, the expectations are more specific than that.

Service-level agreements (SLAs) as discussed in this book are not about legal or contractual agreements between a company and its customers. Rather, they are agreements between teams and service owners. They provide a mechanism for communicating expectations between services.

What are Service-Level Agreements?

Service-level agreements are a *commitment to provide a given level of reliability and performance.*

They are used to create a strong contractual relationship between service owners and consumers.

An overnight delivery service, for example, might have an SLA that states it will deliver a package before 9 a.m. the next morning. An airline might have an SLA expressing its ability to deliver baggage within a certain period of time after a flight arrives. A power company might have an SLA that states how fast it will fix power outages after a storm.

Example 18-1. What are SLAs?

Consider the online store application illustrated in Figure 16-4.

Your customers expect the store to be operating when they want to use it—they expect it to be highly available. They also expect that the site will load fast so that they can use it without delay. Further, they expect the products they want to be available in your store. They expect you to have them in stock and available for shipment. Finally, they expect that when they place an order, the order will show up on their doorstep in a reasonable period of time.

Each of these can be expressed as an SLA. For example:

Availability

Customers expect the store to be operational when they need it. You can express this as a minimum percentage of time that your store is operational. An example availability SLA might be, "Our store will be available at least 99.4% of the time."

Load time

Customers expect the web page to load fast—that is, they want the website to appear responsive. There are many ways you can express this, but in the simplest way, it can be expressed as the maximum amount of time a page will take to load —for instance, "Pages will load within 4 seconds 99% of the time" (see "Top Percentile SLAs" on page 137).

Products

Customers expect the products they want to be available in your store. They also expect those products to be in stock and ready for shipment. You might express this as a percentage, such as "A minimum of 80% of our products in the catalog are in stock."

Shipment

Customers expect the products they order to arrive quickly. You might express this as the time from order until the product is shipped, or as the amount of time until a product appears on the customer's doorstep. As an example, "We ship all products within 24 hours."

All of these are examples of SLAs. Although they are all quite different in nature and meaning, they all fundamentally have the same purpose. They express an expectation of your application by your customers.

You can measure the actual performance of each of these things as your application runs and interacts with customers. You might generate charts and graphs that show your measurements over time. But the SLA is the agreed limit at which your service can be considered performing as expected. The chart in Figure 18-1 shows your store's performance on product in stock, which is a measure of the percentage of the products that are in stock at any given point in time.

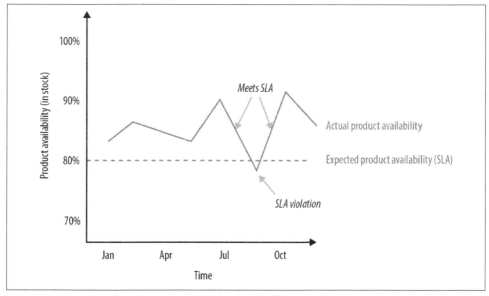

Figure 18-1. Example performance compared to SLA

You can see from the chart that your in-stock percentage varies over time. You can also see your SLA line, representing your expected performance of 80%.

Most of the time, your in-stock percentage is above the SLA (we say we are *meeting our SLA*). However, one time in late summer it dropped below our 80% SLA for a short period of time (we say we *failed our SLA*).

In certain industries, businesses have contractual agreements with customers that require them to meet established SLAs, perhaps with financial or other consequences for failing to meet them.

Amazon Web Services, for example, has SLAs with its customers, and in some cases provides financial compensation if they fail to meet those SLAs.

For example, with Amazon EC2 instances, if AWS's monthly uptime percentage falls below 99.95%, it gives a service credit of 10% to affected customers. If it falls below 99.0%, AWS gives a service credit of 30%. You can find more details of how AWS calculates this SLA and the credit at *https://aws.amazon.com/ec2/sla/*.

Having SLAs for monitoring the ability of your application to perform for your customers can be useful for your internal business uses (making sure you perform as expected for your customers). Or, as AWS does, SLAs may be used for making financial commitments to customers. In either case, the SLA and the way you measure performance against the SLA is identical.

External Versus Internal SLAs

Example 18-1 and the AWS example all demonstrate the use of external SLAs. These are SLAs we might specify and monitor describing how our application performs to our customers.

But SLAs can and should be used between individual services within your application. Here, you can use them as mechanisms for communicating expectations and requirements between the owners and operators of individual services.

Why Are Internal SLAs Important?

Internal SLAs are critically important to the health and maintainability of complex multiservice systems. Why? Well, put simply, how can a service meet its commitments to its customers if the services it depends on are not meeting their commitments? See Chapter 15 for more information.

How can you provide a 50 ms response to your customer when a service you require gives you a 90 ms response?

How can you provide a 99% availability when a service you require only provides a 90% availability?

SLAs as Trust

SLAs are about building trust in a highly distributed and scalable way. When you trust a dependency can meet its expectations, you can set your own service's expectations with confidence.

Example 18-2. Building trust

Consider the online store application illustrated in Figure 16-4. Imagine you and your team owned the price & shipping cost calculator service. Your customers are the website frontend service and the checkout service. One of the primary operations they depend on you for is to look up the price of a product given the product number. Because these services use this to generate web pages for display to end customers, they need the price lookup to be fast. Your team makes an agreement to provide the price lookup uniformly within 20 ms of the request.

Now, for you to meet this commitment, you realize you need to have fast access to the catalog storage service, which contains the data you need to calculate the price. However, given your 20 ms commitment, you are concerned whether the catalog storage service will be able to provide you the data you need fast enough. The catalog storage service is owned by another team. How can you be sure that team will be able to meet your performance requirements? You have two choices.

The first choice is to contact the owning team and look deeply into how their service works, looking for performance issues and problems. Then, analyze the team to make sure you trust they will be able to perform as you need. This, of course, is highly intrusive, very expensive, and not practical for a large organization.

The second choice is to negotiate with the owning team and agree on a performance SLA for their service. Suppose that you work with the team and they agree to a 10 ms response. You know that if they can respond that fast, you can meet your own 20 ms guarantee to your customers.

As long as they can perform to their SLA, you can perform to your SLA.

You can monitor the team's performance against their SLA over time to see how well they do. If the team consistently meets their SLA, you have grown trust in your dependency, and you can now focus your energies on *your* service and what you need to do to ensure that you can continue to meet your 20 ms guarantee to your customers.

SLAs for Problem Diagnosis

SLAs also provide a way of determining where problems exist in a complex system. If a service is experiencing problems, one of the first things to check is whether its dependencies are meeting their SLA expectations. If a dependent service is not meeting its expectations, this becomes a great spot to begin looking to diagnose the problem with your service.

Example 18-3. Finding a problem

Consider the online store application illustrated in Figure 16-4. Imagine that you and your team owned the price & shipping cost calculator service, as described in Example 18-2.

Now, suppose that you receive a call in the middle of the night. Your service has become sluggish in generating price lookups, and it's affecting your company's customers. You check your performance compared to your 20 ms performance guarantee. You find that you are now taking, on average, 500 ms for each lookup. This has substantially slowed your company's storefront, and your customers are dissatisfied.

But, what caused the problem? Is there something wrong in your service? Or is it one of your dependencies that is having the problem?

It could be your service is having some problem—perhaps with its hardware, perhaps something else. But, before you spend a lot of time trying to figure out what is wrong with your service, you check the performance of your dependencies.

Knowing that your service depends on the catalog storage service and that you have a 10 ms SLA guarantee with them, you check their performance against this SLA. You see that they, too, are having a performance problem. Rather than taking less than 10 ms, calls to their service are taking over 400 ms. Obviously, that team is experiencing a performance problem. You check and you find their oncall is already engaged and working on this problem.

Realizing this is the likely cause of your performance problem, you begin tracking the other team's progress toward resolving their problem. This makes more sense than spending valuable time fruitlessly trying to figure out what's wrong with your service.

By having well-defined SLAs with all your service dependencies, you can much more easily track when your service is having a problem or when a dependent service is having a problem.

Performance Measurements for SLAs

There are many measures of performance that services can use, and the specific measures used can and should vary based on the service consumer and owner's needs and requirements. Here are some example types of performance measures:

Call latency
> This is a measure of how long a service call takes to process a request and return a response. Typically measured in milliseconds or microseconds, it is important for the consumer of a service to know how long it takes for a request to be processed, because that time will be part of the total the consumer takes to process its request. This is the type of SLA used in Example 18-2 and Example 18-3.

Traffic volume
> This is a measure of how many requests a service can handle over a period of time. Typically measured in requests/second, a service owner must know how much traffic to expect from a consumer in order to meet its expectations.

Uptime
> This is a measure of how much time a service is expected to be up, healthy, and free of major problems. Typically calculated as a percentage, it is a measure of how available the service has been over a specified period of time (typically day, month, or year).

Error rates
> This is a measure of how many failures a service generates over a period of time. Typically measured as a percentage, it is normally the number of failed requests divided by the total number of requests processed over a given time period.

Limit SLAs

A *limit SLA* typically specifies an operational limit that is expected to be met. If actual performance is better than this limit, we have *met our SLA*. If actual performance is worse than this limit, we have *failed our SLA*. The limit itself is the value of the SLA.

For example, "call rate must be < 1,000 reqs/sec", specifies a limit SLA on the expected traffic volume of a service.

As another example, "request response will be < 20 ms" specifies a limit SLA on the expected call latency of a service.

You can apply a limit SLA to most types of performance measures.

Top Percentile SLAs

Limit SLAs are great when you can measure a value and have a guarantee that the value stays better than that limit at all times. These types of SLAs are great for expressing availability, uptime, and error rates.

Another type of SLA measurement is the *top percentile SLA*. You use it to measure performance of an event when the actual performance of that event typically varies considerably.

Top percentile SLAs are great for measuring things like call latency. The amount of time a request to a service takes to generate a response can vary wildly, and most of the time we don't care if *every* request can be handled in less than a specific period of time, just that *most* requests are handled in less than a specific period of time.

A top percentile SLA is expressed as a percentage of the total data points that are above/below a specific value. The SLA is usually written like this:

```
TP<percentage> is less than <value>
```

Here's an example:

```
TP90 is less than 20msec
```

This can be read as "90% of all request will take less than 20 ms."

Often, we will calculate the performance for an event, such as the call latency to a service, and express it as an actual top percentile for the service, as described in Example 18-4.

Example 18-4. Call latency represented as a top percentile

Suppose that we have a service that responds to service calls. Over a period of time, we have observed the following latency for these service calls:

Service Call Latency - Actual	
Req Time	**Latency**
T + 1 sec	5 msec
T + 2 sec	10 msec
T + 3 sec	20 msec
T + 4 sec	30 msec
T + 5 sec	15 msec
T + 6 sec	8 msec
T + 7 sec	12 msec
T + 8 sec	45 msec
T + 9 sec	12 msec
T + 10 sec	22 msec
T + 11 sec	4 msec
T + 12 sec	8 msec
T + 13 sec	12 msec
T + 14 sec	15 msec
T + 15 sec	14 msec
T + 16 sec	28 msec
T + 17 sec	21 msec
T + 18 sec	32 msec
T + 19 sec	15 msec
T + 20 sec	22 msec

We can chart these values like so:

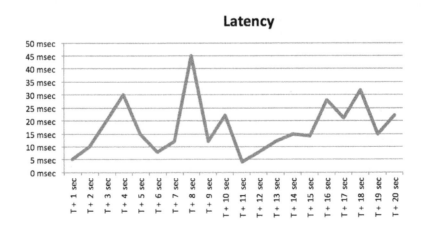

Using this data, we can calculate several *top latency* values for this service:

TP90

> This is the value that 90% of the latency values are below. In this example, 90% of the data is 18 data points. Removing the top 2 data points (45 ms and 32 ms) will leave us with 18 data points, the highest value is 30 ms. So, we can say our *TP90 is 30 ms*.

TP80

> This is the value that 80% of the latency values are below. In this example, that means removing the top 20% (four data points: 45, 32, 30, 28 ms). Of the remaining 16 data points, the highest one remaining is 22 ms. So, we can say our *TP80 is 22 ms*.

Continuing on, here are several TP values representing that data:

```
TP95 = 32 msec
TP90 = 30 msec
TP80 = 22 msec
TP50 = 14 msec
```

There are some other, occasionally useful values to use:

```
TPmax = 45 msec (maximum value)
TPmin = 4 msec (minimum value)
TPavg = 18 msec (average value)
```

The top percentiles of course can change over time. After you have it calculated, you can use a limit SLA to define expectations. For instance, in Example 18-4, your service might have the following SLA:

```
TP90 < 35msec
```

If it did, the service would have met its SLA. However, if it had committed to the following SLA:

```
TP80 < 20msec
```

the service would not be meeting its SLA (the current TP80 is 22 ms). So, the service would have failed its SLA.

Latency Groups

SLAs sometimes are expressed in groups that are related. For example, a service might be able to guarantee a specific latency, but only if the call volume stays within a reasonable amount. So, an SLA may be expressed as follows:

```
Call Latency TP90 < 25msec when Traffic Volume < 250k req/sec
Call Latency TP90 < 30msec when Traffic Volume > 250k req/sec and < 400k req/sec
```

How Many and Which Internal SLAs?

As you build your service, a question you might ask is, how many internal SLAs should I define for my service?

First, keep the number as low as possible. Understanding the meaning of SLAs and their effect becomes very complicated as the number of SLAs increases.

Ensure that you have covered all critical areas within your service. You should have appropriate SLAs for all major pieces of functionality and especially the areas that are critical to your business.

You should negotiate your SLAs with the consumers of your services, as an *SLA that does not meet a consumer's needs is an irrelevant SLA*. However, as much as possible, *use the same SLA for all consumers*. Your service should have, as much as possible, a single set of SLAs that should meet the needs of all your consumers. Having a set of SLAs created per-consumer adds significantly to your complexity, and doesn't provide any real benefit.

You should only specify SLAs that you can actually monitor and alert on. There is no value in specifying an SLA if you cannot validate whether you are hitting it. Additionally, you care if your service violates the SLA, because this should be a leading indicator of a problem, so make sure you receive an alert when an SLA is being violated.

You might want to monitor and alert on values over and above those that you report as internal SLAs. This data can be useful in finding and managing problems in your service without actually being a committed value to your consumers.

You should build a dashboard that contains all of your SLAs and monitors so that you can see at a glance if you are experiencing any problems, and you should make this dashboard available to all your dependencies so that they can see how well your service is performing.

Additionally, ensure that you have access to the dashboards for all of your dependent services, so you can monitor whether they are having problems, which might or might not be affecting your service.

Additional Comments on SLAs

Monitoring and using SLAs can quickly become overwhelming, and you can easily become caught up in the minute details of SLA monitoring.

Perfect, all-inclusive SLA monitoring is not our goal. Having a number you can use to compare is the goal. Any number is better than no number. The purpose of internal SLAs is not to add up numbers, but to provide guidance for you and your dependencies, and to help set expectations between teams appropriately.

SLAs can, and should, become part of a language you use when talking to other teams.

CHAPTER 19

Continuous Improvement

If your application is successful, you'll need to scale it to handle larger traffic volumes. This requires more novel and complicated mechanisms to handle this increased traffic, and your application quality can suffer under the increased burdens.

Typically, application developers don't build in scalability from the beginning. We often think we have done what was necessary to let our application scale to the highest levels we can imagine. But, more often than not, we find faults in our application that make scaling to larger traffic volumes and larger datasets less and less possible.

How can we improve the scalability of our applications, even when we begin to reach these limits? Obviously, the sooner we consider scalability in the lifecycle of an application, the easier it will be to scale. But at any point during the lifecycle, there are many techniques you can use to improve the scalability of your application.

This chapter discusses a few of these techniques.

Examine Your Application Regularly

Parts I and II provided extensive coverage on maintaining a highly available application and managing the risk inherent in the application. Before you can consider techniques for scaling your application, you must get your application availability and risk management in shape. Nothing else matters until you make this leap and make these improvements. If you do not implement these changes now, up front, you will find that as your application scales, you will begin to lose touch of how it's working and random, unexpected problems will begin occurring. These problems will create outages and data loss, and will significantly affect your ability to build and improve your application. Furthermore, as traffic and data increases, these problems simply become worse. Before doing anything else, get your availability and risk management in order.

Microservices

In Part III, we discussed service- and microservice-oriented architectures. Although there are many different architectural decisions you need to make and architectural directions you need to set, make the decision early to move away from a monolithic or multimonolithic architecture and move instead to some form of a service-oriented architecture.

Service Ownership

While you move to a service-based architecture, also move to a distributed ownership model whereby individual development teams own all aspects of the services for which they are responsible. This distributed ownership will improve the ability of your application to scale to the appropriate size, from a code complexity standpoint, a traffic standpoint, and a dataset size standpoint. Ownership is discussed in greater detail in Chapter 15.

Stateless Services

As you build and migrate your application to a service-based architecture, be mindful of where you store data and state within your system.

Stateless services are services that manage no data and no state of their own. The entire state and all data that the service requires to perform its actions is passed in (or referenced) in the request sent to the service.

Stateless services offer a huge advantage for scaling. Because they are stateless, it is usually an easy matter to add additional server capacity to a service in order to scale it to a larger capacity, both vertically and horizontally. You get maximum flexibility in how and when you can scale your service if your service does not maintain state.

Additionally, certain caching techniques on the frontend of the service become possible if the cache does not need to concern itself with service state. This caching lets you handle higher scaling requirements with fewer resources.

Where's the Data?

When you do need to store data, given what we just discussed in the preceding section, it might seem obvious to store data in as few services and systems as possible. It might make sense to keep all of your data close to one another to reduce the footprint of what services have to know and manage your data.

Nothing could be farther from the truth.

Instead, localize your data as much as possible. Have services and data stores manage only the data they need to manage to perform their jobs. Other data should be stored in different servers and data stores, closer to the services that require this data.

Localizing data this way provides a few benefits:

Reduced size of individual datasets
> Because your data is split across datasets, each dataset is smaller in size. Smaller dataset size means reduced interaction with the data, making scalability of the database easier. This is called *functional partitioning*. You are splitting your data based on functional lines rather than on size of the dataset.

Localized access
> Often when you access data in a database or data store, you are accessing all the data within a given record or set of records. Often, much of that data is not needed for a given interaction. By using multiple reduced dataset sizes, you reduce the amount of unneeded data from your queries.

Optimized access methods
> By splitting your data into different datasets, you can optimize the type of data store appropriate for each dataset. Does a particular dataset need a relational data store? Or is a simple key/value data store acceptable?

Data Partitioning

Data partitioning can mean many things. In this context, it means partitioning data of a given type into segments based on some key within the data. It is often done to make use of multiple databases to store larger datasets or datasets accessed at a higher frequency than a single database can handle.

There are other types of data partitioning (such as the aforementioned functional partitioning); however, in this section, we are going to focus on this key-based partitioning scheme.

A simple example of data partitioning is to partition all data for an application by account, so that all data for accounts whose name begins with A–D is in one database, all data for accounts whose name begins with E–K is in another database, and so on (see Figure 19-1).[1] This is a very simplistic example, but data partitioning is a common tool used by application developers to dramatically scale the number of users who can access the application at once as well as scale the size of the dataset itself.

---

[1] A more likely account-based partitioning mechanism would be to partition by an account identifier rather than the account name. However, using account name makes this example easier to follow.

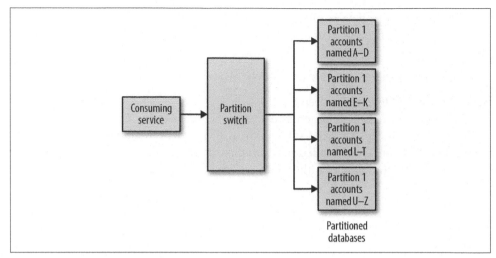

Figure 19-1. Example of data partitioning by account name

In general, you should avoid data partitioning whenever possible. Why? Well, whenever you partition data this way, you run into several potential issues:

- You increase the complexity of your application because you now have to determine where your data is stored before you can actually retrieve it.

- You remove the ability to easily query data across multiple partitions. This is specifically useful in doing business analysis queries.

- Choosing your *partitioning key* carefully is critical. If you chose the wrong key, you can skew the usage of your database partitions, making some partitions run hotter and others colder, reducing the effectiveness of the partitioning while complicating your database management and maintenance. This is illustrated in Figure 19-2.

- Repartitioning is occasionally necessary to balance traffic across partitions effectively. Depending on the key chosen and the type and size of the dataset, this can prove to be an extremely difficult task, an extremely dangerous task (data migration), and in some cases, a nearly impossible task.

In general, account name or account ID is almost always a bad partition key (yet it is one of the most common keys choosen). This is because a single account can change in size during the life of that account. An account might begin small and can easily fit on a partition with a significant number of small accounts. However, if it grows over time, it can soon cause that single partition to not be able to handle all of the load appropriately, and you'll need to repartition in order to better balance account usage. If a single account grows too large, it can actually be bigger than what can fit on a single partition, which will make your entire partitioning scheme fail, because no rebalancing will solve that problem. This is demonstrated in Figure 19-2.

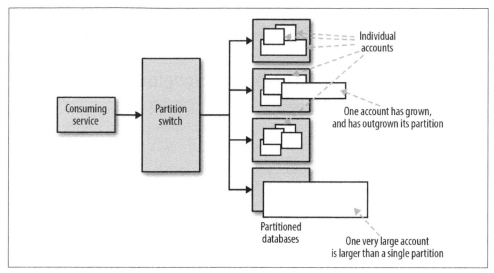

Figure 19-2. Example of accounts overrunning data partitions

A better partition key would be one that would result in consistently sized partitions as much as possible. Growth of partitions should be as independent and consistent as possible, as shown in Figure 19-3. If repartitioning is needed, it should be because all partitions have grown consistently and are too big to be handled by the database partition.

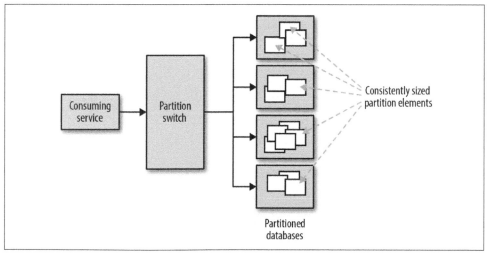

Figure 19-3. Example of consistently sized partitioned elements

One potentially useful partitioning scheme is to use a key that generates a significant number of small elements. Next, map these small partitions onto larger partitioned databases. Then, if repartitioning is needed, you can simply update the mapping and move individual small elements to new partitions, removing the need for a massive repartitioning of the entire system.[2]

The Importance of Continuous Improvement

Most modern applications experience growth in their traffic requirements, in the size and complexity of the application itself, and in the number of people working on the application.

Often, we ignore these growing pains until the pain reaches a certain threshold before we attempt to deal with it. However, by that point, it is usually too late. The pain has reached a serious level and many easy techniques to help reduce the growing pains are no longer available for you to use.

By thinking about how your application will grow long before it grows to those painful levels, you can preempt many problems and build and improve your applications so that they can handle these growing pains safely and securely.

---

2 Selecting and utilizing appropriate partition keys is an art in and of itself, and is the subject of many books and articles.

PART V

Cloud Services

Today's forecast: "cloudy with a chance of scaling…"

CHAPTER 20

Change and the Cloud

Cloud computing has changed the way we think about building and running our applications. But, while how we build applications has changed around the cloud, the cloud itself has changed, and the way we think about the cloud has changed as well.

What Has Changed in the Cloud?

The cloud has matured over the past decade. Cloud providers have increased their product offerings. They no longer simply provide file storage and compute capacity. AWS provides 50 unique service offerings to meet a variety of computing needs.

So, what are the biggest changes the cloud is bringing to us and our applications? The following sections outline some key changes.

Acceptance of Microservice-Based Architectures

As we have discussed in this book, service- and microservice-based architectures have grown in popularity in recent years. Migrating applications to some form of a service-based architecture is becoming a standard technique in reducing technical debt and making applications easier to maintain.

As companies look toward moving their applications to the cloud, they are moving to the cloud usually as part of an overall product modernization strategy. This modernization strategy includes moving to state-of-the-art application architectures. In recent years, this state-of-the-art application architecture involves using microservices and other service-based architectures as part of that strategy. This is because technologies such as Docker have made microservice-based architectures a viable technology for application development.

Realizing this, cloud providers have begun to provide higher-value managed offerings, such as the EC2 Container Service, for use in managing our microservice-based containers.

Smaller, More Specialized Services

As we modernize our applications and move them to the cloud, we begin looking at cloud services and how they can be utilized as extensions to our application's services. Capabilities historically provided within the applications are now provided by the cloud.

The major cloud providers now provide features such as databases, caching services, queuing services, logging services, content delivery network (CDN) capabilities, and transcoding services.

Greater Focus on the Application

The cloud has created a shift in focus away from the creation and management of the infrastructure needed to run our applications, and let us spend our time on more critical aspects of the application and the application environment. The cloud has largely removed a major hurdle in application management, making it possible for us to focus our attention on higher-value aspects of running our applications.

The Micro Startup

The cloud has made it possible for very small startups, often self-funded, single-person operations, to come into existence leveraging the inexpensive and scalable computing and other technology capabilities that the cloud offers.

It has never been easier for an individual with an idea to build that idea and potentially profit from it. The ability to build a compute ecosystem without the need to invest in an expensive infrastructure is helping to get new, fresh ideas to come to market quickly. In particular, mobile applications such as online games have benefited greatly from this capability.

These startups bring applications online quickly that either flourish or fail, with minimal investment. For those that flourish, the cloud gives the applications the means to scale easily and inexpensively, letting companies invest in infrastructure at a rate proportional to their business needs. This has made it a lot easier to run and manage small startup companies financially.

Security and Compliance Has Matured

In the early days of the cloud, security issues were often cited as one of the primary reasons why companies could not move their applications to the cloud.

Recoginizing the need for improved security, cloud providers now provide better capabilities for securing cloud applications. Cloud companies also have added security assurances in the form of regulatory compliances such as PCI, SOC, and HIPPA.

Combined with a strong track record of visible high-quality security, these changes have removed security as an obstacle for a company looking to consider moving to the cloud.

Change Continues

Change is inevitable. The cloud has changed how we think about building and running our applications. We have begun building smaller, more specialized services. We have learned how to handle larger and larger quantities of data. We focus less on our application's infrastructure and more on our applications. Smaller companies have become more viable, bringing fresh new ideas and insights into our world. And security has become standard in everything we do.

The cloud has matured and caused our use and interactions with the cloud to mature. This will continue into the future, and we must constantly adapt to keep up with the changing landscape. Only then, can our applications continue to grow and expand.

Good, bad, or otherwise, the cloud has changed and continues to change us all.

CHAPTER 21

Distributing the Cloud

We all know the value of distributing an application across multiple data centers. The same philosophy applies to the cloud. As we put portions of our applications, or complete applications, into the cloud, we need to watch *where* in the cloud they are located. How distributed our applications are is just as important in cloud approaches as it is with normal data centers, particularly as applications scale.

However, the cloud makes knowing *whether* your application is distributed more difficult. The cloud also makes it more difficult to proactively make your application more distributed. Some cloud providers don't even expose enough information to let you know where, geographically, your application is running.

Luckily, larger providers like AWS, although they won't tell you specifically where your application is running, will give you enough information to make decisions about where your application is running. Interpreting and understanding this information and using it to your advantage requires an understanding of how AWS is architected.

AWS Architecture

First, let's discuss some terms used within the AWS ecosystem.

AWS Region

An AWS region is a large area connection of cloud resources that represent a specific geographic area. In general, regions represent a portion of an individual continent or country (such as Western Europe, Northeastern Asia-Pacific, and United States East). They describe and document *geographic diversity* of cloud resources. They are composed of multiple *availability zones* (AZs); however, it is possible for a region to have only a single availability zone.

An AWS region is identified by a string representing its geographical location. Table 21-1 gives the current list of AWS regions, their names, and where they serve.

Table 21-1. AWS regions

Region name[a]	Geographic area covered
us-east-1	US East Coast (N. Virginia)
us-west-1	US West Coast (N. California)
us-west-2	US West Coast (Oregon)
eu-west-1	EU (Ireland)
eu-central-1	EU (Frankfurt)
ap-northeast-1	Asia Pacific (Tokyo)
ap-northeast-2	Asia Pacific (Seoul)
ap-southeast-1	Asia Pacific (Singapore)
ap-southeast-2	Asia Pacific (Sydney)
sa-east-1	South America (Sao Paulo)

[a] AWS regions and availability zones as of February 2016.

AWS Availability Zone

An AWS availability zone is a subset of an AWS region that represents cloud resources within a specific portion of a region but are network topologically isolated from one another. AWS availability zones describe and document *network topological diversity* of cloud resources. If two cloud resources are in different availability zones, they can be assumed to be in distinct data centers, even if they are in the same AWS region. If two cloud resources are in the same availability zone, they can potentially both be in the same data center, floor, rack, or even physical server.

An AWS availability zone is identified by a string beginning with the name of the region the AZ is in, followed by a letter (a–z). For example, Table 21-2 shows some example availability zones and the regions they are in.

Table 21-2. AWS availability zone names

Region name	AZ names
us-east-1	us-east-1a us-east-1b us-east-1c us-east-1d us-east-1e
us-west-1	us-west-1a us-west-1b
us-west-2	us-west-2a us-west-2b

Data Center

This is not a term used within AWS vocabulary, but we will use it as we map typical noncloud terminology into AWS terminology.

A data center is a specific floor, building, or group of buildings that constitute a single location of system resources, such as servers.

Architecture Overview

Figure 21-1 shows at a high level what the AWS cloud architecture looks like. AWS is composed of several AWS regions, which are geographically distributed around the globe in order to provide high-quality access to most locations in the world. The AWS regions each have connections to the Internet. The AWS regions themselves also are connected among themselves, but they use long-distance network connections similar to the rest of the Internet.

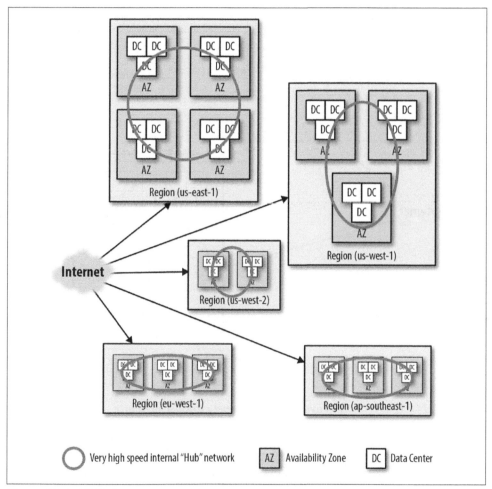

Figure 21-1. AWS data center architecture

A single AWS region is composed of one or more AWS availability zones. The AZs within a single region are connected via an extremely high-speed hub network link, as shown in Figure 21-2. The goal is to make access between any two servers within a region to have similar performance characteristics without concern for the AZ in which they are located.

A given AZ is composed of one or more data centers, depending on the size of the AZ.

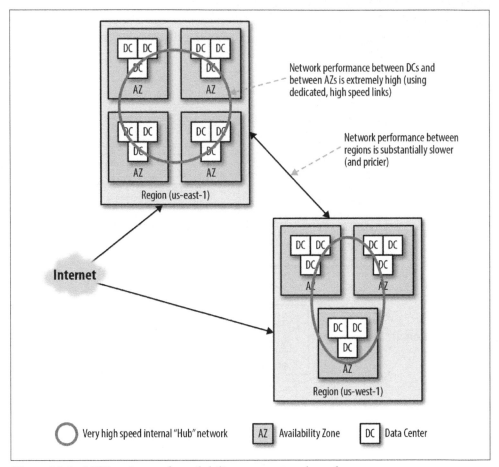

Figure 21-2. AWS region and availability zone network performance

As you can see, the network topography is designed to make it easy to build an application within a single region but distributed across availability zones. This distribution is designed to give redundant systems failover opportunities in light of problems with individual data centers, while maintaining the ability for the independent components to communicate with one another at high speeds transparently, without regard to the availability zone they are in.

However, regions are designed so that an entire application would be contained within a single region, and not require high-speed communications with components contained in other regions. Instead, if an application wants to be in multiple regions, multiple copies of the application are typically run independently, one copy within each region desired. This makes it possible for individual geographic regions to have access to an instance of an application locally without suffering the cost of long-distance communication links. This is shown in Figure 21-3. This model is supported by the AWS network traffic costing model, which typically allows traffic between AZs within a single region to be free, while traffic destined between regions or out from a region to the Internet to be charged appropriately.

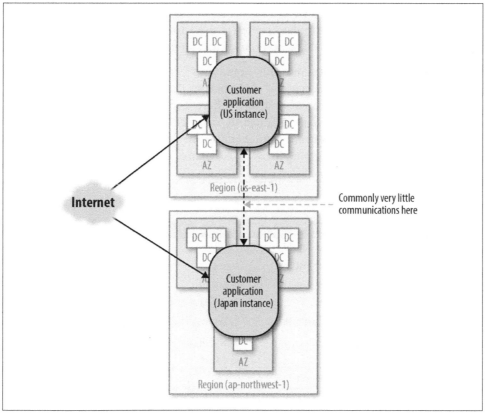

Figure 21-3. Customer architecture

This architecture is important not only from a cost standpoint, but also from a latency standpoint (region-to-region network latency is higher than AZ-to-AZ).

Additionally, this structure gives your application the ability to support various governmental regulations, such as EU Safe Harbor.[1]

Availability Zones Are Not Data Centers

Within a given account, an EC2 instance in one AZ (such as us-east-1a) and an EC2 instance in another AZ (such as us-east-1b) may safely be assumed to be in distinct data centers.

However, this is not necessarily true when you are using more than one AWS account. When you create an EC2 instance in account 1 that is in AZ us-east-1a, and an EC2 instance in account 2 that is in AZ us-east-1c, these two instances might, in fact, be on the same physical server within the same data center.

Why is this the case? It is because the AZ names do not statically map directly to specific data centers. Instead, the data center(s) used for "us-east-1a" in one account might be different than the data center(s) used for "us-east-1a" in another account.

When you create an AWS account, they "randomly" create a mapping of availability zone names to specific data centers.[2] This means that one account's view of "us-east-1a" will be physically present in a very different location than another account's view of "us-east-1a". This is demonstrated in Table 21-3. Here we show an arbitrary number of data centers (arbitrarily numbered 1 through 8) within a single region. Then, we show a possible mapping between AZ names and those data centers for four sample accounts.

Table 21-3. Unexpected availability zone mappings

Data Center	AWS Account 1	AWS Account 2	AWS Account 3	AWS Account 4	...
DC #1	us-east-1a	us-east-1d		us-east-1e	...
DC #2	us-east-1a	us-east-1c	us-east-1a	us-east-1a	...
DC #3	us-east-1b	us-east-1a	us-east-1d	us-east-1d	...
DC #4	us-east-1c		us-east-1a	us-east-1b	...
DC #5	us-east-1d	us-east-1b	us-east-1c	us-east-1c	...
DC #6	us-east-1e		us-east-1b		...
DC #7			us-east-1e		...
DC #8		us-east-1e			...

---

1 EU Safe Harbor is a set of EU privacy principles that govern the transmission of data about EU citizens to locations outside of the EU. It often can matter where data is stored in order to comply with local laws, and AWS regions make it possible for applications to be built to support these laws and principles.

2 Of course, it's not random, but done algorithmically. And actually the mapping is not done until a specific account makes use of a specific availability zone or region.

From this, you'll notice a few things. First, a single AZ for an account can, in fact, be contained in multiple distinct data centers. This means the two EC2 instances you create within a single account and a single AZ may be on the same physical server, or they could be in completely different data centers. Second, two EC2 instances created in different accounts may or may not be in the same data center, even if the AZs are different.

For example, in Table 21-3, if account #1 creates an instance in us-east-1b, and account #3 creates an instance in us-east-1d, those two instances will both be created in data center #3.

This is important to keep in mind for one simple reason: *just because you have two EC2 instances in two accounts in two different AZs, does not mean they can be assumed to be independent for availability purposes.*

As discussed in Parts I and II of this book, maintaining independence of replicated components is essential for availability and risk management purposes. However, when using multiple AWS accounts, the AWS AZ model does not enforce this. The AZ model can be used to enforce this only when dealing within a single AWS account.

Why would you ever want to use more than one AWS account? Actually, this is fairly common. Many companies create multiple AWS accounts used by different groups within the company. AWS might do this for billing purposes, permissions management, or other reasons.

Ever Wonder Why They Do This?

Ever wonder why, when AWS announces an outage, they will say that an outage impacts "some availability zones" in a given region, but they do not say which ones?

The reason is because of how the system is mapped: if they have a problem in, say DC#4, that might mean your "us-east-1a," whereas for the next person it might be "us-east-1c." They cannot give the name of a specific AZ, because the name of the AZ is different for each account.

Why does AWS use this weird mapping? One of the main reasons is for load balancing. When people launch EC2 instances, they tend not to launch them evenly distributed across all availability zones. In fact, "us-east-1a" is a more common AZ for people to launch EC2 instances than "us-east-1e." This is governed as much by human nature as anything. If AWS did not do this artificial remapping, AZs *earlier* in the alphabet would be overloaded, whereas AZs *later* in the alphabet would be less loaded. By creating this artificial mapping, they are able to load balance usage more effectively.

Maintaining Location Diversity for Availability Reasons

How do you ensure that AWS resources you launch have redundant components that are guaranteed to be located in different data centers and therefore risk tolerant to outages?

There are a couple things you can do. First, make sure that you maintain redundant components in distinct AZs within a single account. If you have redundant components that are in multiple accounts, make sure you maintain redundancy in multiple AZs within each account individually. Don't compare AZs across accounts.

CHAPTER 22

Managed Infrastructure

When you think of the cloud, what do you think of? If you are like most people, you think of the following:

- File storage (such as Amazon S3)
- Servers (such as Amazon's Elastic Compute Cloud, or EC2)

And, in fact, you can utilize the cloud efficiently and effectively using only these two resources.

However, cloud companies offer a wide variety of managed services that you can take advantage of to ease your management load, increase your availability, and even improve your scalability.

Knowing how these components are organized and managed can help in determining which capabilities you wish to utilize for your application.

Structure of Cloud-Based Services

There are three basic types of cloud-based services:

- Raw resource
- Managed resource (server-based)
- Managed resource (non-server-based)

Figure 22-1 illustrates these three types.

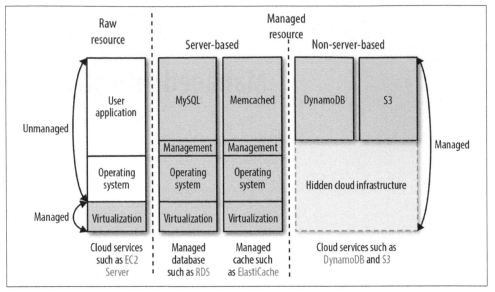

Figure 22-1. Types of cloud-based services

Raw Resource

A raw cloud resource provides basic capabilities to the user and provides only basic management.

An example of a raw cloud resource is Amazon EC2, which provides raw server capabilities in a managed manner.

The cloud provides management of the basic server virtualization layer, and the creation of the instance and its initial filesystem. However, after the instance is up and running, the operation of the server itself is opaque to the cloud provider.

The cloud provider manages the data flowing into and out of the instance (the network), as well as the CPU and the utilization of the CPU. But the provider does not know anything about what is running within the server itself, nor does it monitor anything that goes on in the server.

For companies like Amazon, this is intentional. What runs on the server is your business, and Amazon does not want to be responsible for any aspect of the software running on it. Amazon's *line of responsibility* ends at the entry/exit points to the virtual server itself.

You can see the impact of this in a couple different ways. For EC2 instances, look at the metrics that Amazon collects and provides to you via CloudWatch:

- How much network traffic is going into the instance

- How much network traffic is leaving the instance
- How much data is read from the disks
- How much data is written to the disks
- The amount of CPU that is being consumed

But missing from this list are some obviously useful metrics that it does not track:

- Amount of free memory (they do not know how the memory is used)
- Amount of disk space free (they do not know the structure of the data on the disks)
- Number of processes running (they do not know what a process is on the server)
- Memory consumed by applications (they do not know what an application is)
- Swap or paging activity (they do not know how memory is allocated or managed)
- Which process are consuming the most resources (they do not know what a process is)

For another example, look at access control to the instance. There are two types of access controls that are in place with a typical server:

The network access control list (ACL)
Access control provided at the network (firewall) layer.

User identification
Access control to identify users who can log in and access capabilities on the server.

Amazon manages the network ACL throughout the life of the instance (they call them security groups). You can change the security group ACLs at any time. If you block access to a port, that port is blocked immediately. If you allow access to a port or IP address, that port or IP address is allowed access immediately. This all happens at the network layer, before the traffic reaches the server for inbound ACL, and after the traffic leaves the server for outbound ACL. No access to software on the server itself is required.

But user identification is different. When the server is first set up, you can specify a keypair (public/private access key) that will be installed on the instance. This keypair provides the user initial access to the server using appropriate software on the instance, such as SSH.[1] However, as soon as the instance has launched, Amazon has no further way to add or remove user identificiation access to the instance. You can't

---

1 For a Linux OS, it is SSH, but the specific software depends on the OS and software installed on the image.

add new key pairs, nor remove key pairs from the access list. All of that is controlled from the (unmanaged) software running on the server. In the case of a Linux kernel, it is in SSH configuration files on the operating system.

What about software upgrades? If your software needs to be upgraded on the server, it is your responsibility to ensure that happens. Amazon has no ability to manage that for you.

Amazon manages everything up to the server boundary, but provides no management of anything that goes on within the server itself.

Managed Resource (Server-Based)

A server-based managed resource is a resource that provides a full stack managed solution for a specific cloud capability.

For instance, a managed database solution might run the database and special management software on an existing managed server, making it possible for the entire stack, server and software on the server to be managed by the cloud provider.

A great example of a server-based managed resource is Amazon's Relational Database Service (RDS) database capability. This service provides a complete managed database solution, such as a MySQL database, within a managed service.

Take a look at Figure 22-1 again, and you can see how RDS is structured. Basically, when you launch an RDS instance, you launch an EC2 instance that is running a specific OS, special management software, and the database software itself. Amazon manages not only the EC2 server, but the entire software stack as well, including the OS and database software.

You can see the impact of this by looking at the CloudWatch metrics provided by RDS instances. Besides the basic EC2 instance information, you get additional monitoring about the database itself, such as the following:

- Number of connections made to the database
- Amount of filesystem space the database is consuming
- Number of queries being run on the database
- Replication delay

These are metrics only available from the OS or the database software itself.

Another way to understand the impact is to consider the type of configuration you can perform. No longer is the configuration just basic information about the server (network connections and disks connected)—you can also configure information about the database itself, such as maximum number of connections, caching information, and other configuration and tuning parameters.

Additionally, software upgrades are now managed as part of the cloud layer. If an upgrade is required for the database software, that upgrade is managed by Amazon for you.

Managed Resource (Non-server-based)

Non-server-based managed resources are resources that provide a specific capability, but do not expose the server infrastructure the capability is running on.

A great example of a non-server-based managed resource is Amazon S3. This service provides cloud-based file storage and transmission. When you store a file in S3, you communicate directly with the S3 service. There is no *server* or *servers* that are allocated on your behalf to perform the actions. The fact that there might be one or more servers[2] running behind the scenes to perform the request is invisible to you.

The entire operation is managed, but you only have visibility and the ability to control the exposed software interface provided by the service (in the case of S3, that is uploading files, downloading files, deleting files, and so on). You have no visibility nor ability to control the underlying operating system or the servers that service is running on. These servers are shared among all users of the service, and as such are managed and controlled by Amazon without your involvement.

Implications of Using Managed Resources

When a service or a part of a service is managed, there are many advantages for you, the user of the service. Here are some in particular:

- You do not need to install or update the software of a managed system.
- You do not need to tune or optimize the system (but you may have some capabilities to do so via the cloud provider).
- You do not need to monitor and validate that the software is performing as expected.
- The cloud provider can provide monitoring data for you to consume, if you desire, without additional software or capabilities.
- The cloud provider can provide backup and replication capabilities for the service.

---

2 Or in the case of S3, many, many servers.

There are disadvantages to managed components:

- You typically do not have the ability to significantly change how the software performs its operations.
- You do not have the ability to control when and how the software is upgraded, or the version of software that is running.[3]
- You are limited to the capabilities offered by the cloud provider for monitoring and configuring the service.

Implications of Using Non-Managed Resources

When a service or a part of the service is non-managed, there are also some advantages for you, the user of the service. Here are some in particular:

- You can control what software is running on the service, what version is running, and how it is set up.
- You control when and how upgrades are performed, or if they are performed.
- You can monitor and control the software in whatever manner you want, using whatever mechanisms you want.

There are disadvantages to non-managed components:

- Nothing is free. You are completely responsible for all management and maintenance that the system requires.
- You must make sure you perform your own backup and data replication.
- You must monitor your software to ensure that it is functioning correctly—if you do not, no one will let you know when it fails.
- If the software breaks or fails, you alone are responsible for fixing it. The cloud provider cannot help.

Monitoring and CloudWatch

I often get the question, "Is CloudWatch sufficient for monitoring my cloud resources?" The answer I give is a resounding "no."

---

3 However, the cloud provider can provide you some of these capabilities; for example, RDS provides a range of database versions that it supports, but not all versions are available. In managed systems like S3, you have no control over the software upgrade process at all.

Why? Because CloudWatch only provides monitoring capabilities for those components that Amazon manages. This means it provides really good coverage for monitoring things like DynamoDB as well as server-based managed resources such as RDS and ElastiCache.

But for EC2 servers, CloudWatch provides only baseline information for monitoring the low-level server and the server virtualization. It does not provide any monitoring or alerting for anything above the server virtualization.

To monitor your EC2 servers completely, you need two additional things:

- A server/operating-system monitor that monitors the OS and the server from within the server. This provides information such as memory utilization, swapping, and filesystem usage.

- An application performance monitoring solution that monitors your application from within the application. This will provide information about how the application is performing, how users are using the application, and information on errors and problems that occur within the software.

Only with all three of these monitoring capabilities (the previous two and Cloud-Watch) can you consider an EC2 server completely monitored.

CHAPTER 23

Cloud Resource Allocation

To effectively and efficiently utilize cloud resources, you need to understand how they are allocated, consumed, and charged. Cloud resources can be divided reasonably into these two categories:

- Allocated-capacity resources
- Usage-based resources

Allocated-Capacity Resource Allocation

Allocated-capacity resources are cloud resources that are allocated in discrete units. You specify how much of a specific type of resource you need, and you are given that amount. This amount is *allocated* to your use, and you are allocated that amount independent of what your real needs are at the moment.

Allocated-capacity cloud resources can be recognized by the following characteristics:

- They are allocated in discrete units.
- You specify how many units you want, and they are allocated for your use.
- If your application uses less of the resource, the allocated resources remain idle and unused.
- If your application needs more of the resource, the application becomes resource starved.
- Proper capacity planning is important to avoid both over and under allocation.

The classic example of allocated capacity cloud resources are servers, such as Amazon EC2 instances. You specify how many instances you want as well as the size of the servers, and the cloud allocates them for your use. Additionally, managed infrastructure components such as cloud databases[1] use an allocated capacity model. In all of these cases, you specify the number of units and their size, and the cloud provider allocates the units for your use.

But there are other examples of capacity-allocated cloud resources that operate a bit differently—for example, Amazon DynamoDB is one. Using this option, you can specify how much capacity you want available for your DynamoDB tables. In this case, capacity is not measured in units of *servers*, but in units of *throughput capacity units*. You allocate how much capacity you want to provide to your tables, and that much capacity is available for your use to that table. If you don't use that much capacity, the capacity goes unused. If your application uses more than the capacity you have allocated, your application will be resource starved until you allocate more capacity. As such, these *capacity units* are allocated and consumed in a manner very similar to *servers*, even though on the surface they look very different.

Changing Allocations

Typically, capacity is allocated in discrete steps (a server costs a certain amount per hour; DynamoDB capacity units cost a certain amount per hour). You can change the number of servers allocated to your application or the number of capacity units allocated to your DynamoDB table, but only in discrete steps (the size of your server or the size of a capacity unit). Although there can be steps of various sizes available (such as different server sizes), you must allocate a whole number of units at a time.

It is your responsibility to ensure that you have enough capacity at hand. This might involve performing capacity planning exercises similar to those that you perform for traditional data center–based servers. You may very well allocate capacity based on expected demand and leave the number alone until you perform a review and determine that your capacity requirements have changed. This is typical of non-cloud-based server allocation.

However, cloud allocation changes are easier to perform than traditional capacity changes in a data center. As such, other algorithms can be used to perform your allocation. For instance, because allocation changes can be typically performed (almost) immediately, you can wait until you have consumed (almost) all your capacity before you decide to increase your capacity allocation.

Another option available is to change your allocation on a fixed schedule that matches your use patterns. For instance, increase the number of servers available during heavily used daylight hours and decrease the number of servers during lesser-used nighttime hours.

---

1 Such as Amazon RDS, Amazon Aurora, and ElastiCache.

Yet another option is to change your allocation dynamically and automatically, based on current usage patterns. You might, for instance, monitor CPU usage on your servers and as soon as their usage reaches a certain threshold, you can automatically allocate additional servers.[2] You might build these automated mechanisms into your application or your service infrastructure yourself, or you might take advantage of cloud services such as AWS's AutoScaling to automatically change your allocation based on current usage criteria that you specify.

Whatever mechanism you choose to determine and change capacity, it is important to note that whatever capacity you currently have allocated is all that is available to you, and you could still end up with capacity allocated (and charged) to you that is not being used. Even worse, you could find yourself resource starved because you do not have enough capacity. Even if you use an automated allocation scheme such as AutoScale to give your application additional capacity when it is needed, that does not mean that the algorithm AutoScale uses to change your capacity can notice the need fast enough before your application becomes resource starved by, for instance, a sudden resource usage increase.

Allocation Problems

Consider Amazon's Elastic Load Balancer (ELB). This is a service that provides a load balancer to your application that automatically scales in size to handle whatever quantity of traffic has been sent to it. If you are receiving very little traffic, ELB will change the servers it is using for your load balancer to be smaller servers and fewer of them. If you are receiving a lot of traffic, ELB will automatically change the servers used for your load balancer to be larger servers and put more of them into service. All of this is automatic and transparent to you as the application owner. This is how ELB is able to provide a load balancer at a very low entry price point, yet let the same load balancer scale to handle huge quantities of traffic (with a corresponding price increase) all automatically. This saves you money when your traffic is light, yet scales to your higher traffic needs when necessary.

However, there are places where the specifics of how this automated allocation mechanism becomes visible in a negative way. If you receive a sudden spike in traffic, say, because your site suddenly goes viral due to a social media campaign, your load balancer might not be able to resize itself fast enough. The result? For a period of time after the traffic increase starts, your load balancer might be resource starved, causing page requests to be slow or fail, creating a poor user experience. This situation will automatically correct as ELB determines your increased capacity needs and scales your load balancer up to larger servers and more of them. This scaling, though, can

---

2 Or, in reverse, remove servers when CPU usage drops below a threshold.

take a few minutes to complete. In the meantime, your users are having a poor experience and availability suffers.

To combat this effect, Amazon lets you contact representatives and warn them of a coming change in traffic use patterns, allowing them to *prewarm* your load balancer.[3] This effectively means prescaling your load balancer to use larger servers (and more of them), before the traffic spike occurs. However, this only works if you know you will experience a sudden rise in traffic. It doesn't help at all if the traffic spike is sudden or unexpected.

This situation is one of the problems with this type of cloud resource allocation.

Whether you change allocations manually or via an automated method, your usage is defined and constrained by your allocation. You pay for the entire allocation, whether you use it or not. If your application requires a higher allocation than is currently allocated, your application will be resource starved. Proper capacity planning, either manual or automated, is essential for managing these resources.

Reserved Capacity

You typically can change your allocated capacity as often as you want,[4] increasing and decreasing as your needs require.

This is one of the advantages of the cloud. If you need 500 servers one hour and only 200 the next hour, you are only charged for 500 for one hour and 200 for the next hour. It's clean and simple.

However, because of this essentially infinite flexibility in the amount of capacity you can allocate, you pay a premium price.

But what if your needs are more stable? What if you will *always* need at least 200 servers allocated? Why pay for the ability to be flexible in how many servers you need on an hour-by-hour basis when your needs are much more stable and fixed?

This is where *reserved capacity* comes into play. Reserved capacity is the ability for you to commit to your cloud provider up front that you will consume a certain quantity of resources for a period of time (such as one to three years). In exchange, you receive a favorable rate for those resources.

---

3 For more information, see "Best Practices in Evaluating Elastic Load Balancing." (*http://amzn.to/28Jgwjz*)

4 There are sometimes restrictions, such as on DynamoDB, for which there are limitations to how often you can change capacity.

Example 23-1. Reserved Capacity Example

Reserved capacity does not limit your flexibility in allocating resources; it only guarantees to your cloud provider that you will consume a certain quantity of resources.

Suppose that you have an application that requires 200 servers continuously, but sometimes your traffic spikes so that you need to have up to 500 servers allocated at times. You can use AutoScale to automatically adjust the number of servers dynamically. Your usage in servers, therefore, varies from a minimum of 200 servers to a maximum of 500 servers.

Because you will always be using at least 200 servers, you can purchase 200 server's worth of reserved capacity. Let's say you purchase 200 servers for one full year. You will pay a lower rate for those 200 servers, but you will be paying for those servers all the time. That's fine, because you are using them all the time.

For the additional 300 servers (500 – 200), you can pay the normal (higher) hourly rate, and only pay for the time you are using those servers.

Reserved capacity provides a way for you to receive capacity at a lower cost in exchange for committed allocation of those resources.[5]

Usage-Based Resource Allocation

Usage-based resources are cloud resources that are not allocated but are consumed at whatever rate your application requires. You are charged only for the amount of the resource you consume. There is no allocation that is required.

You can recognize usage-based cloud resources by the following characteristics:

- There is no allocation step involved, and hence no capacity planning required.
- If your application needs less resources, you use fewer resources and your cost is lower.
- If your application needs more resources, you use more resources and your cost is higher.
- Within reason, you can scale from a very tiny amount consumed to a huge amount consumed without taking any steps to scale your application or the cloud resource it is consuming.

---

[5] Using reserved capacity also guarantees that the specific type of instance will be available in your specific desired availability zone, when you want it. Without having reserved capacity, it is possible that you could request a specific type of instance in a specific availability zone, and AWS would not be able to honor the request.

- The phrase "within reason" is defined entirely by the cloud provider and their abilities.

You typically have no visibility into how the resources are allocated or scaled. It is all invisible to you.

A classic example of usage-based cloud resources is Amazon S3. With S3, you are charged for the amount of data you are storing and the amount of data you transfer. You do not need to determine ahead of time how much data storage you require or how much transfer capacity you require. Whatever amount you require (within system limits) is available to you whenever you require it, and you pay only for the amount you use.

The "Magic" of Usage-Based Resource Allocation

These services are easy to manage and scale because no capacity planning is required. This seemingly "magic" materialization of the resources necessary for your application using a usage-based resource is one of the true benefits of the cloud. It is made possible by the multitenant nature of the cloud service.

Behind a service like Amazon S3 is a huge amount of disk storage and a huge number of servers, which are allocated as needed to individual requests from individual users. If your application has a spike in the amount of resources it requires, the necessary resources can be allocated from a shared *availability pool* of services.

This availability pool is shared by *all* customers, and so it is a potentially huge pool of resources. As your application's resource spike ebbs, another user's application might begin to spike, and those resources are then allocated to that user's application. This is done completely transparently.

As long as the pool of available capacity is large enough to handle all the requests and all the resource usage spikes occurring across all users, there is no starvation by any consumer. The larger the scale of the service (the more users that are using the service), the greater the ability of the cloud provider to average out the usage spikes and plan enough capacity for all the users' needs.

This model works as long as no single user represents a significant portion of the total resources available by the cloud provider. If a single customer is large enough to represent a significant portion of the resources available for the service by the cloud provider, that customer can experience resource starvation during peak usage and potentially affect the capacity available to other customers, as well.

But for services like Amazon S3, the scale of the service is so massive,[6] that no single customer represents a significant portion of usage, and the resource allocation of S3 remains *magical*.

 However, even Amazon S3 has its limits. If you run an application that uses significant quantities of data transferred or stored, you can run into some of the limits S3 imposes in order to keep from causing other users from experiencing resource starvation. As such, a large consumer of S3 resources can reach these artificial limits and experience resource starvation itself. This typically happens only if you are talking about data storage and transfer in the petabyte range.

Even if you do consume S3 resources at these huge levels, there are ways you can move your usage around to reduce the impact of the limits. Additionally, you can contact Amazon and request that these limits be increased. They will increase those limits in specific areas as you require, and these limit increases are then fed into Amazon's capacity planning process so they can ensure that there are sufficient resources available to meet your needs and everyone else's.

The Pros and Cons of Resource Allocation Techniques

As outlined in Table 23-1, each of the techniques we've been discussing have some advantages and disadvantages.

Table 23-1. Cloud resource allocation comparison

	Allocated-capacity	Usage-based
Service examples (Amazon AWS)	EC2, ELB, DynamoDB	S3, Lambda, SES, SQS, SNS
Requires capacity planning	Yes	No
Charges based on	Capacity allocated	Capacity consumed
Under utilization	Capacity is idle	N/A
Over utilization	Application starved	N/A
Can capacity be reserved to save money?	Yes	No
How can capacity be scaled?	Manual or scripted allocation change; can be delayed	Automatic and immediate

---

6 According to the most recent published Amazon data I could find, in 2013 S3 stored two trillion objects. That's five objects for every star in the Milky Way. See "Amazon S3 – Two Trillion Objects, 1.1 Million Requests / Second," (*http://amzn.to/28Jw1HJ*) AWS Official Blog, April 18, 2013.

	Allocated-capacity	Usage-based
How are usage spikes handled?	Potential usage starvation during spike or capacity ramp-up	Handled transparently
Excess capacity?	Allocated and saved for your use	Global pool available for any customer to use

CHAPTER 24

Scalable Computing Options

Setting up, configuring, and managing servers, and deploying your applications to them, is only one way of deploying your high-scale application. There are other alternatives, each with a different set of advantages and disadvantages. In this chapter, we'll discuss various alternatives, from cloud-based servers to AWS Lambda and talk about how they differ, how they are the same, and how to decide which to choose for your application's needs.

In this chapter, we compare various cloud-based[1] application execution environments, specifically:

Cloud-based servers
> This is basic server technology. Examples include Amazon EC2 servers.

Compute slices
> These are traditional software applications running in compute environments independent of servers. Examples include Heroku Dynos and Google App Engine.

Dynamic containers
> Full server capabilities wrapped in the ability to quickly start, stop, and migrate to new systems. Docker is the best example of this.

Microcompute
> Small size, highly scaled, event-driven execution environments. AWS Lambda is the best example of this.

---

1 Some of these techniques apply to non-cloud-based deployment environments, but because our discussion is focused on scalability, we'll examine scalable cloud-based uses only.

Before we compare these methods, let's look at each of them individually.

Cloud-Based Servers

Cloud-based servers are the simplest way to acquire scalable computing, and are the most consistent with traditional programming and system architecture models. Cloud-based servers are available everywhere, with Amazon EC2 instances being the most popular and best-known example.

The primary benefit of using cloud-based servers is their ability to be quickly brought online and utilized, which is especially useful for scaling. However, they require an application to be constructed in such a way that adding additional servers to a deployment can actually improve the application scalability. Although this might be true in many environments for many applications, it is not universally true.

Advantages

- Least expensive option per compute cycle
- Very few limits on functionality; most server capabilities are available
- Run continuously

Disadvantages

- Allocated capacity.[2] Scaling is about provisioning new servers and deploying an application to that server.
- You pay for allocated capacity, not used capacity.
- Application architecture must support scalability by allowing additional servers to be brought online.
- Many advantages of standalone servers cannot be utilized effectively in a scaled environment (such as local storage capabilities).
- The server must be managed and maintained by the application owner, including software and security upgrades.

Optimized Use Cases

Cloud-based servers are good for a wide variety of general-purpose use cases and can be utilized for most scaling needs.

---

2 See Chapter 23 for a discussion of the pros and cons of allocated capacity.

Compute Slices

Compute slices are an alternative execution model that involves executing applications without knowledge of which server they are running on. They involve taking an application's software and deploying it to a Platform-as-a-Service (PaaS) infrastructure that will execute the stack in a managed way. This is done without exposing the specifics of the server on which software is running.

There are several examples of compute slice–based compute engines, but Heroku Dynos is a classic example.

Advantages

- Easy to vary allocated capacity at a relatively granular scale.
- Providers of compute slices have a strategy of over-provisioning of slices. This facilitates potentially lower per-slice cost points, which is especially useful for low-traffic applications.
- No server management required.

Disadvantages

- More expensive per-compute cycle than cloud-based servers.
- Allocated capacity. Scaling is about provisioning new slices to run your application.
- You pay for allocated capacity, not used capacity.
- You have no control over the server and infrastructure components that are being utilized.

Optimized Use Cases

A traditional use case is a low-traffic web application.

It's most effective where a traditional application or service needs to be run, but the owner does not want to deal with managing servers or other infrastructure requirements.

In applications for which usage is relatively low and a small number of slices can run the entire application, slices can provide a cost-effective option. However, the larger the application, the more costly it is compared to basic servers.

It should be noted that Google App Engine is another example of compute slice–based programming and provides similar advantages/disadvantages to what we just described, except their payment mechanism is different and allocation is handled more dynamically. The point here is that many of the advantages and disadvantages of slice-based computing depend on the implementation, not the general concept.

Dynamic Containers

Dynamic containers is a specific use case of container technology that involves dynamically allocating and migrating containers to different servers to provide a highly scaled, managed compute environment. Note that containers can be utilized as a deployment technology in any of these compute environments. What we are speaking about here is a dynamic model for easily moving and scheduling containers to optimize system resources and make adding new containers easy.

In a dynamic container environment, an application, wrapped in a container, is designed to be easily started, stopped, and relocated quickly and easily. Combined with a microservice-based application architecture, dynamic containers can provide a highly dynamic and fluid application that can be scaled easily and effectively, and existing compute resources can be optimized more effectively than with traditional compute or more static container deployment strategies.

Advantages

- Inexpensive and easy to effectively optimize existing server capabilities.
- Scaling is easier because containers can be deployed dynamically wherever compute resources are available.
- Containers place few limits on the application with the exception, perhaps, of slow application startup time, which can negatively affect advantages of container scheduling).
- Containers can run either continuously or only when needed, conserving resources.
- Containers are easy to deploy and servers require minimum configuration for them to be utlized.
- Starting up new services in an environment is easy and can be automated.

Disadvantages

- Requires active container management and software for managing container deployment and scheduling. Some cloud providers have services that help with this, but it is still a relatively new field and no single solution for managing dynamic containers has proven to be better than other approaches. The sweet spot in container scheduling and management has not yet been realized.

Optimized Use Cases

Dynamic containers are great for easy deployment of complex applications in a microservice-based architecture. They also are great for rapidly starting and stopping service instances (container start/stop is very similar in scope to starting/stopping a Linux process).

Microcompute

Microcomputing is the pinnacle of scalable compute technology. Microcomputing is a compute model wherein a relatively simple (micro) piece of code is available to execute, and is run whenever necessary in response to some incoming event, such as a user request or a service call. Each event causes a single execution of the microcompute function to run and act on the event. An arbitrary number of microcompute functions can be executing independently at a time, handling all incoming requests as they occur. This effectively provides a nearly limitless scaling runtime environment. AWS Lambda is the best example of microcompute technology.

Microcompute is similar to the compute slice model of program execution. The biggest difference is that compute slices are allocated and scheduled in discrete units. You can change the number of running discrete units to handle incoming requests, but ultimately your ability to scale to the number of incoming requests is limited by your ability to scale-up discrete compute slices. Microcompute is scaled completely dynamically with the number of instances running only a function of the current number of requests to process.

To make this possible, compute functions used within Lambda must be small, nimble, and require virtually no initializtion or destruction to execute effectively.

Advantages

- Automatic and near limitless scaling as needed[3]
- No server management, no system upgrades
- Charges based on actual number of events processed; limited overhead
- Easily supports rapidly changing scaling needs (scale up/down is transparent)

---

3 Obviously it is not limitless scaling, but for any given practical application needs, it can be considered near limitless.

Disadvantages

- Significantly limited functionality and languages.

- Applications must be architected around the use of the microcompute technology.

- Most expensive on a per-compute-cycle basis, but pricing models and the ability to charge at a very granular basis can help with this.

- Current implementations (AWS Lambda) do not provide good deployment, rollback, or A/B testing capabilities, making them more difficult to utilize in a highly available application without additional application architecture or external tooling.

Optimized Use Cases

Microcompute is optimized for high-volume data streaming and event processing. It is useful for data validation, transformation, and filtering. On the network edge, it is useful for validation and regulation of inbound data.

This is most effectively used when small operations utilizing a small code base is necessary to perform specific event-based programming.

Now What?

With the wide variety of scalable compute options available now, almost any application and IT operational need can be successfully met by one or more of the available alternatives.

But how do you determine which one you should use? Many of these techniques are available only on specific cloud providers. As such, the availability and desire to use these compute options may be a piece of your cloud provider selection process.

Still, almost any major cloud provider can support many of these options, which is one of the advantages the cloud offers today. Don't be afraid to use multiple options within your application, as different parts of your application will often have different needs. As always, consider your application's availability and scalability needs, and pick the solutions that best match the needs of your application and the teams that support that application.

CHAPTER 25

AWS Lambda

AWS Lambda is a new software execution environment created by AWS designed to provide event-driven compute capabilities without the need to purchase, set up, configure, or maintain servers. Lambda gives you virtually unlimited scalability with the ability to pay at a subsecond-metered level.

Lambda is a great technology for background processing of event-triggered actions. Here are some typical use cases:

- Image transformation for newly uploaded images
- Real-time metric data processing
- Streaming data validation, filtering, and transformation

It is best suited for any sort of processing where:

- Operations need to be performed as the result of an event occurring in your application or environment
- A data stream needs filtering or transformation
- Edge validation or regulation of inbound data is necessary

But the real power of Lambda is that it completely removes the concerns around scalability. Lambda can scale to almost any rational scaling size necessary, without any actions required to make that happen.

Using Lambda

At this point, you might be thinking "Sounds great, but what are some architectures that can utilize Lambda?" The following sections describe some of these.

Event Processing

Consider a picture management application. Users can upload pictures to the cloud, which are then stored in S3. The application displays thumbnail versions of those pictures and lets users update attributes associated with those pictures, such as name, location, names of people in the picture, and so on.

This simple application can utilize AWS Lambda to process images after they are uploaded to S3. When a new picture is uploaded, a Lambda function can be automatically triggered that takes the picture and creates a thumbnail version of that picture and stores the thumbnail version in S3. Additionally, a different Lambda function can take various characteristics about the picture (such as size, resolution, etc.) and store that metadata in a database. The picture management application can then provide capabilities for manipulating the metadata in the database.

This architecture is shown in Figure 25-1.

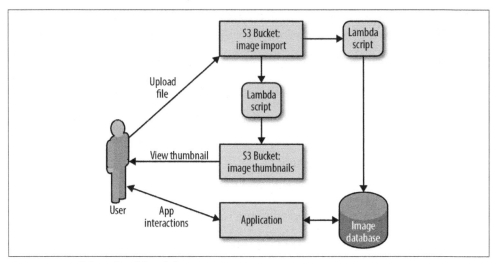

Figure 25-1. File upload lambda usage

The picture management application does not need to be involved in the file upload process at all. It can rely on standard S3 upload capabilities and the two Lambda functions to do all processing necessary to complete the file upload process. So, the picture management application only has to deal with what it is good at: manipulating metadata in the database for existing pictures.

Mobile Backend

Consider a mobile game that stores user progress, trophies, and high scores in the cloud, making that data available for a shared community as well as device portability for individual users.

This application involves a series of APIs on the backend that are created so that the mobile application can store data in the cloud, retrieve user information from the cloud, and then perform community interactions.

The necessary APIs are created by using an API Gateway[1] that connects with a series of Lambda functions. The scripts perform the operations necessary, in conjunction with some form of database, to handle the cloud backend for the mobile game.

This architecture is shown in Figure 25-2.

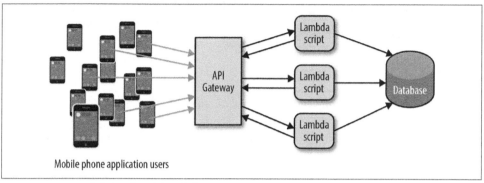

Figure 25-2. Mobile backend lambda usage

In this model, no servers are needed on the backend, and all scaling is handled automatically.

Internet of Things Data Intake

Consider an application that takes data from a huge quantity of data sensors deployed around the world. Data from these sensors arrives regularly. On the server side, this results in an enormous quantity of data being regularly presented to the application for storage in some form of data store. The data is used by some backend application, which will be ignored for this example. The data intake needs to validate the data, perhaps perform some limited processing, and store the resulting data into the data store.

This is a simple application that only performs basic data validation and verification and stores the data in a backend data store for future processing. However, although the application is simple, it must run at a massive scale, in the order of millions or billions of data intake events per minute. The exact scale is dependent on the number of sensors.

---

1 The Amazon API Gateway is an API creation service that is designed to work with AWS Lambda.

This architecture makes use of a data intake pipeline[2] that sends data to an AWS Lambda function that performs any necessary filtering or processing of the data before it's stored in the data store.

This architecture is shown in Figure 25-3.

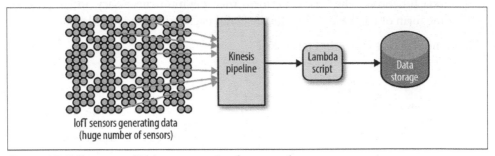

Figure 25-3. Internet of Things sensor intake example

Lambda is well suited to handling the huge volume of data that must be ingested at a high speed regularly.

Advantages and Disadvantages of Lambda

AWS Lambda has one primary advantage: scale. Lambda is very good at handling massive scale loads without the need to increase the amount of infrastructure allocated to your application.

It accomplishes this by requiring the code that is run to be extremely simple in nature, allowing it to be easily spun up on multiple servers in multiple stacks quickly and effectively, on an as-needed basis.

This is Lambda's sweet spot: small code footprint executed at mammoth scale.

So, where should you not use Lambda? To answer that, let's look at the disadvantages of Lambda:

- Implicit coding requirements (simple, event driven, fast processing)
- Complex configuration and setup
- No native built-in staging or testing environments
- No native deploy/rollback capabilities
- No native A/B capability testing
- No development environment for building and testing Lambda functions

---

2 Amazon Kinesis is a real-time streaming data intake pipeline designed to handle the intake of vast data streams.

In short, Lambda is great for scaling small scripts, but it is poor at all of the other things necessary for a large-scale application deployment.

Used effectively, AWS Lambda is a technology that will significantly help in your extreme scaling needs. However, be careful to limit its use only to those tasks for which it is well suited. For compute execution needs outside of the AWS Lambda sweet spot, use other deployment/execution options.

PART VI

Conclusion

Architecting for scale is about more than just handling large numbers of users.

CHAPTER 26

Putting It All Together

We have covered a lot of material in a lot of different topics in this book that, when taken together, are designed to help you scale your applications:

- Availability and availability management
- Risk and risk management
- Building applications by using services and microservices
- Scaling your application and your development team to work on your application
- Using the cloud to help scale your application

Availability

Availability is the ability of your application to perform the tasks it is capable of doing. This differs from reliability, which is the ability of your application to not make mistakes. A system that adds 2 + 3 and returns 6 has poor reliability. A system that adds 2 + 3 and never returns a result has poor availability.

Poor availability is caused by many things, including the following:

- Resource exhaustion
- Unplanned load-based changes
- Increased number of moving parts
- Outside dependencies
- Technical debt

Application availability is often the first casualty as an application tries to scale beyond its capabilities. The topic of availability is covered extensively in Part I, including how to measure it and how to maintain a highly available application. Even in light of continuously increasing scaling needs, your application availability can be maintained at appropriate levels for your needs.

Risk Management

You cannot possibly manage the risk in your system if you cannot identify the risk in your system. This is the critical lesson from Part II. Understanding your risk is the first and most important step in operating a highly available, highly scalable application.

After you understand your risk, you must manage that risk. Although removing risk is always desirable, often the cost of doing so is unacceptably high, both from an actual cost standpoint, and from an opportunity cost to your application. You certainly have more important, more customer-focused things to do that are better for your customers, your company, and your bottom line than to remove every ounce of risk you know from your application.

Instead of removing all risk, you must manage the risk. This involves evaluating two values with every risk, the risk's *likelihood*, and the risk's *severity*. These two values are so important, we dedicated all of Chapter 6 to the subject. Generally, severity is the cost to you if a risk happens, whereas likelihood is the chance of the risk happening.

A risk that can cause a very serious problem in your application (but is virtually impossible to happen) might not be one that you want to try and remove. Similarly, a risk that is highly likely to happen, but would have very little impact on your application, is probably not a risk you will need to prioritize removing. Yet a risk that is somewhat likely to happen and can cause a reasonably serious problem may, in fact, be the most important risk for you to work on resolving.

We introduced a tool called the *risk matrix*, which can be quite effective in helping you manage the risks of your application and determine which risks need to be mitigated or removed.

We discussed techniques for mitigating risk, techniques for validating mitigation action plans, and techniques for building applications with reduced risk.

Services

A service is a distinct enclosed system that provides business functionality in support of building one or more larger products. Services provide an application architecture pattern that facilitates building systems in a manner that promotes improved system and development team scalability.

When building highly scaled applications, services provide the ability to make improved scaling decisions, accommodate improved team focus and control, reduce complexity at the local level, and improve testing and deployment capabilities.

We provided tools and suggestions for how to build high availability into your application at the service level, and reduce the effect of service failures on your application and its users.

Scaling

We covered how to build your scaling plans to ensure system availability and management. We discussed building systems "two mistakes high" to avoid failure loops and cascading dependencies.

We also looked at the Single Team Owned Service Architecture paradigm, or STOSA. This provides a model for scaling your development organization as your application scales, to provide the ability for a larger number of engineers to effectively work on a single application, without sacrificing application scalability or availability. This involves defining what it means to be a service owner and organizing your application around these principles.

We talk about using tools for managing service dependencies to maintain application quality even during times of hyper growth, including internal SLAs and service tiers.

Cloud

Finally, we looked at the cloud and how you can use it to build highly scaled applications.

We looked at how the cloud has changed the way we think about computing, and the way we think about building applications. We discussed building geographic and network topographical diversity into your application using the cloud, and how to avoid pitfalls where you believe your application is geographic and network topological diverse, when in fact it might have built-in dependencies that increase your risk of problems.

We addressed the use of managed infrastructure and how you can utilize it in highly scaled applications. We covered how cloud-based resources are allocated, and the role you need to play in ensuring that your applications have the cloud resources they need to keep operating.

We then discussed compute options available to you when using the cloud. We looked at AWS Lambda, and the revolutionary future in scalable development it enables.

Architecting for Scale

Architecting an application for scalability is more than building an application that handles lots of users at the same time. There are many things involved in making an application scalable:

- You must be able to handle a large and growing number of customers.
- You must be able to handle a large and growing quantity of data used by your customers.
- You must be able to handle a growing complexity in what your customers want to accomplish with your application.
- You must be able to add more developers working on your application as your company's needs expand, and you must do so without sacrificing development speed, efficiency, or application quality.
- You must keep your application online and functioning, even in light of all of the aformentioned changes and improvements.

These aren't easy problems to solve. The techniques discussed in this book are designed to help you solve these and many more of your application scalability concerns.

Index

A

acceptable availability, 16
alerts, 13, 140
allocated-capacity resources, 171-175
    allocation problems, 173
    changing allocations, 172-174
    reserved capacity, 174
    usage-based vs., 177
Amazon
    raw cloud resource management, 164-166
    RDS, 166
Amazon API Gateway, 187
Amazon DynamoDB, 172
Amazon EC2, 164
    as allocated capacity resource, 171
    AZ vs. data centers with, 160-161
    monitoring and CloudWatch, 169
    SLAs, 133
Amazon Elastic Load Balancer (ELB), 173
Amazon Kinesis, 188
Amazon S3, 167
    Lambda and, 186
    limits of, 177
    usage-based allocation, 176
Amazon Web Services (see AWS)
API contracts, 74
API Gateway, 187
application availability (see availability)
applications
    building with failure in mind, 8
    building with scaling in mind, 9
    distributing across the cloud, 155-162
    effects of growth, xv
    guidelines for separating into services, 76-82

    service-based, 70-71
automated change management, 20-23
    configuration management, 22
    deploys, 21
    repeatable tasks, 21
    sanity test for, 23
    scaling, 24
    system improvement, 24
automation
    manual processes, 20-23
    operational processes, 65
    server rebooting, 66
AutoScaling, 173
availability, 193
    acceptable, 16
    automation of manual processes, 20-23
        (see also automated change manage-
            ment)
    basics, 3-6
    before implementing scaling, 143
    building applications with failure in mind, 8
    building applications with scaling in mind, 9
    causes of poor, 5
    defined, 5
    expressed as percentage, 15
    factoring maintenance windows into, 17
    icon failure example, 7
    improvement after slippage in, 19-24
    improvement techniques, 7-14
    maintaining AWS location diversity for, 162
    measuring, 15-17
    measuring/tracking current percentage, 20
    monitoring as feature of application design,
        12

About the Author

Lee Atchison is the Principal Cloud Architect and Advocate at New Relic. He's been with New Relic for four years where he designed and led the building of the New Relic infrastructure products, and helped New Relic architect a solid service-based system architecture that scales as they have grown from a simple SaaS startup to a high traffic public enterprise. He has a specific expertise in building highly available systems.

Lee has 28 years of industry experience, and learned cloud-based, scalable systems during his seven years as a Senior Manager at Amazon.com. At Amazon, he led the creation of the company's first software download store, created AWS Elastic Beanstalk, and led the team that managed the migration of Amazon's retail platform from a monolith to a service-based architecture.

Colophon

The animal on the cover of *Architecting for Scale* is a textile cone sea snail (*Conus textile*). It is also known as the "cloth of gold cone" due to the unique yellow-brown and white color pattern of its shell, which usually grows to about three to four inches in length. The textile cone is found in the shallow waters of the Red Sea, off the coasts of Australia and West Africa, and in the tropical regions of the Indian and Pacific oceans.

Like other members of the genus *Conus*, the textile cone is predatory and feeds on other snails, killing their prey by injecting them with venom from a "radula," an appendage that resembles a small needle. The "conotoxin" used by the textile cone is extremely dangerous and can cause paralysis or death.

The textile cone reproduces by laying several hundred eggs at once, which grow on their own into adult snails. Their shells are sometimes sold as trinkets, but the textile cone is plentiful and their population is not threatened or endangered.

Many of the animals on O'Reilly covers are endangered; all of them are important to the world. To learn more about how you can help, go to *animals.oreilly.com*.

The cover image is from *Wood's Illustrated Natural History*. The cover fonts are URW Typewriter and Guardian Sans. The text font is Adobe Minion Pro; the heading font is Adobe Myriad Condensed; and the code font is Dalton Maag's Ubuntu Mono.

Get even more for your money.

Join the O'Reilly Community, and register the O'Reilly books you own. It's free, and you'll get:

- $4.99 ebook upgrade offer
- 40% upgrade offer on O'Reilly print books
- Membership discounts on books and events
- Free lifetime updates to ebooks and videos
- Multiple ebook formats, DRM FREE
- Participation in the O'Reilly community
- Newsletters
- Account management
- 100% Satisfaction Guarantee

Signing up is easy:

1. Go to: oreilly.com/go/register
2. Create an O'Reilly login.
3. Provide your address.
4. Register your books.

Note: English-language books only

To order books online:
oreilly.com/store

For questions about products or an order:
orders@oreilly.com

To sign up to get topic-specific email announcements and/or news about upcoming books, conferences, special offers, and new technologies:
elists@oreilly.com

For technical questions about book content:
booktech@oreilly.com

To submit new book proposals to our editors:
proposals@oreilly.com

O'Reilly books are available in multiple DRM-free ebook formats. For more information:
oreilly.com/ebooks

Lightning Source UK Ltd.
Milton Keynes UK
UKOW05f0347270816

281570UK00002B/5/P